This book is dedicated to people who
might wish to enjoy the benefits of
life in a condominium and to people
who handle, control and direct the
affairs of a condominium.

WARNING--DISCLAIMER

This book does not lay claim to be an authority on the subjects discussed. There may be better methods, but those presented here have worked well for the author. If you should desire additional information, you would do well to contact your local public library.

Extreme effort has been expended to make the book as accurate as possible. Even so, a few errors may have been overlooked. Any suggestions for improvement will be welcomed by the author.

The author has written to provide information and pleasure. He and Sāgamon Press shall not be liable to anyone for loss said to be caused in whole or in part by information within this book.

If you feel that the above is not agreeable, return the book for a complete price refund.

Withdrawn

CONDOMINIUM LIVING

By John Summersett

What It Is Really Like
to Participate in a Condo

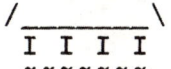
Sagamon Press
Florence, Oregon

CONDOMINIUM LIVING

What It Is Really Like to Participate in a Condo

By John Summersett

Published by:

```
 _____
/        \    Sagamon Press
 I  I  I  I   P.O. Box 2272
 ~~~~~~~      Florence, OR 97439
```

Copyright © 1990 by John Summersett

All rights reserved. No portion of this book may be reproduced without written permission from the publisher except by a reviewer who may quote brief passages in connection with a review.

Library of Congress Catalog Card Number: 91-90010

ISBN 0-9628325-0-2   14.95 Softcover

CONTENTS

CONDOMINIUM LIVING

1   Advantages: 7
Delightful Retirement--Easy Recreation--Closeness to Work, Schools and Shopping Centers--Having Friends Nearby--Being Economical--Owning a Unit and Some Common Area

2   Development: 15
Oregon Revised Statutes (ORS)--Declaration--Bylaws

3   Government: 19
Association Action (Meetings)--Appointed Committees--Board of Directors

4   Management: 29
Bookkeeping--Maintaining Buildings--Maintaining grounds--Administering Problems--Collecting Dues--Choosing Type of Management

5   Insurance: 43
Oregon Revised Statutes (ORS)--Bylaws--Experience at River View Condominium--Insurance Summary

6   Problems: 51
Restitutions--Finances--Bylaws--Common Utilities--Construction--Unit Numbering--Dues--Garbage and Grounds--Leaks--Lateness Penalty--Marina--Meetings--Maintenance--Deferred Maintenance--Roofing Repair--Sea Wall--Arguments--Need for Legal Help--Rentals--Absenteeism--Emergencies--Communicating--Security

7   Bookkeeping: 77
Checkbook--Unit Owner Ledger--Analysis Ledger--Budget--Statement of Expenses and Income--Dues Apportionment Statement--Balance Sheet--Income Tax

8   Living: 95

APPENDIX A
    Oregon Revised Statutes (ORS):   99

APPENDIX B
    Declaration: 121

APPENDIX C
    Bylaws: 131

1
ADVANTAGES

ADVANTAGES

Delightful Retirement--Easy Recreation--Closeness to Work, Schools and Shopping Centers--Having Friends Nearby--Being Economical--Owning a Unit and Some Common Area

People have adopted condominium living with gusto, and the results are pleasing and widespread. Housing, for example, is designed efficiently to accommodate many people in close proximity to each other--housing that is attractive, strong and well-located, whether in urban renewal areas or in new resort areas. Single unit sprawl becomes four-plex or highrise.

Beyond housing, the benefits are seen in every thing you do, where you go and whom you go with. And it's all affordable.

Delightful Retirement

Retirees, especially, like the benefit of a more trouble-free life: no more upkeep of a large home; time to enjoy hobbies like fishing or backpacking, even within walking distance; time to read and watch television. Furthermore, the condominium home is one that can be locked up and forgotten while the owner flies to far-off vacation delights. With many close neighbors the home remains warm and secure.

Last but not least, here you can neatly escape the old rat race and the interminable traffic jams.

Easy Recreation

The recreational advantages of condominiums attract more than just retirees. Many people have them as second homes in resort areas. Sometimes only a week of time is purchased, and still it is less expensive than in other accommodations. Single people find that they can associate closely with others who are congenial, while living close by in their own private and secure homes. Business people buy in just to enjoy clubhouse facilities.

At River View (Condominium) the unit owners enjoy the use of boat slips in a marina adjacent to the condominium--all in a great salmon fishing area on a large estuary and river, five miles from the Pacific Ocean.

In fact, River View is a classic example of how a comdominium can be in the center of superb recreation. Here you find great scenic beauty with full, green forests reaching the ocean's edge along some of America's most beautiful and variable coastline.

Experience hunting and year-round lake and deep-sea fishing in a sportsman's paradise surrounded by countless wilderness campsites--Find seventeen freshwater lakes within a distance of seven miles.

Discover an endless array of water sports like sailing, water skiing, scuba diving and whitewater rafting or dune buggying and three wheeling in the nearby sand dunes of a National Recreation Area. Hike, backpack, or ride horses on trails along the ocean or in the mountains.

Enjoy the abundance of coastal foods--fresh salmon, Dungeness crab, several varieties of clams (some of the best clamming to be found anywhere), rainbow trout, wild blackberries, huckleberries and mushrooms--all of which you can easily catch, dig or pick yourself.

Closeness to Work, Schools and Shopping Centers

Would you like to live only ten blocks from everything you need? You could walk that and get your exercise too. What an advantage! Imagine, a modern shopping center with the finest grocery store, hardware, variety, clothing--This is what we have at River View, and it's what many other condominiums have also.

These condominium homes are deliberately set in areas of peace and quiet--often with a marvelous view--and yet they are close to the hustle and bustle of a vibrant city.

If you ever wanted to ride a bicycle, even as a means of transportation, here is your chance in the quiet streets of a smaller city; shop by bicycle.

Having Friends Nearby

You meet people and make friends in a condominium, again without special effort. This is automatic, because meetings are frequent to ensure the harmonious operation of the association. But the companionship is realized from more than business association: it comes from clubs like travel, bridge, tennis; nights for bingo; special potlucks, breakfasts, dinners; and projects like preparing a float for a parade.

Outside the condominium are friendly, small-city people that beam with civic pride.

Community involvement abounds, and the library is very important.

Being Economical

A big advantage of a condominium is that it costs less. This is so for many reasons, the most obvious being that constructing compact, multiple-story buildings saves both in labor and in materials. The expensive land for the choice location may not even be available to an individual, and, in any case, much less need be bought for a highrise than for sprawling single-family homes.

Other expenses are reduced as a result of pooling for many people, which is the case with utilities, garbage collection and insurance. Maintenance is less for the same reasons that construction costs less.

Insurance is always a large expense, but with condominiums the replacement cost is smaller and the risk is less, so companies charge less.

In the end, when the condominium is finally sold, there is additional gain, because the resale value of condominiums is higher than for other forms of real estate.

Owning a Unit and Some Common Area

Another favor is that the unit owner really owns two different entities: 1. A living space, residence, with title, exclusive. 2. An undivided interest in all the land, buildings, improvements, equipment and reserves that comprise the condominium project, except the privately-owned spaces or units. And the beauty of this is that among these improvements might be a carport or even a swimming pool, both of which the owner can use without painful, personal upkeep.

The unit owner may be more than one person--e.g., man and wife, or a developer group--and along with the other unit owners forms the Association which manages the undivided, commonly-owned project. The principal association considered in the following pages is River View.

2

DEVELOPMENT

DEVELOPMENT

Oregon Revised Statutes (ORS)--Declaration--Bylaws.

At the very beginning of the development of a condominium, sets of rules must be established not only for construction of the buildings and grounds, but also for management and for guiding the conduct of the owners. Usually, this is done through three distinct sets of guidelines. The first (1) is the state law, in our case the Oregon Revised Statutes (ORS), which specifies all the requirements on the developer in an extensive "Declaration". It requires adoption of Bylaws, which it lays out in some detail. Then it provides regulations and requirements for sales of condominium units. Finally, it discusses fraud, deceit and penalties.

State law may require a fourth set of rules to protect the public, a Public Report. These rules are issued by the Real Estate Commissioner to ensure that each developer of a condominium discloses fully and accurately to prospective purchasers all material circumstances or features affecting the condominium, including descriptions of the documents mentioned here or elsewhere that may bind the purchasers.

The second (2) set of guidelines is the declaration itself, in which the developer creates the association. He submits his development to the condominium form of ownership and use in accordance with state law. In this declaration the developer describes the property, the units, the common elements, percentage interests, expenses chargeable to unit owners, adoption of bylaws, and the plan and order of development.

The third (3) set is the bread and butter of the condominium, the guidelines for self management and operation: in other words, the bylaws. Discussed in these laws are the plan of unit ownership, meetings, board of directors, officers, budget and expenses, records, maintenance and use of the condominium and alterations of the bylaws.

These three sets of guidelines applicable to River View Condominium are presented in detail as appendices A, B and C to provide a convenient reference, beginning with the ORS.

Oregon Revised Statutes (ORS)

See Appendix A.

Declaration

See Appendix B.

Bylaws

See Appendix C.

3

GOVERNMENT

GOVERNMENT

Association Action (Meetings)--Appointed Committees--Board of Directors.

The Association of Unit Owners is the governing body for the condominium--a body that governs by it's work at meetings, principally the annual meeting, with the help of committees it creates. Chief among these is the Board of Directors, the work horse of the association.

The association makes and enforces rules in conformance with the bylaws, the declaration and the ORS; but most of the rules are already established in those papers and are carefully watched by the board of directors, which occasionally makes a rule under the watchful eye of the association.

Association Action (Meetings)

The event of the year for this ruling body is the annual meeting, and preparations for it must be made with care and in detail because it happens so rarely and then for only about two hours. It's almost a case of, "speak now or forever hold your peace."

In the first place, the date for the meeting is usually set for July, a convenient date for out-of-state owners. Then, to give the owners plenty of time to think and prepare. the notice of the meeting is sent not more than, say, 60 days nor less than, say, 10 days before the meeting date. Of course, to make sure the owners think about the important items, a tentative agenda is included in the notice, typically as follows:

AGENDA

1. Approval of minutes for August 16, 1988, and September 10, 1988.
2. Consideration and approval of Treasurer's report.
   a. Statement of Expenses and Income to July 1989, and Proposed 1990 Budget. (Phase IV may cause changes).
   b. Dues reduction for advance pay-ment.
   c. Balance Sheet.
3. Consideration of flood insurance for Phases II and III.
4. Approval of owners for $ 10 penalty on late dues; and placement of a lien on any unit that is hopelessly late in making dues payments.
5. Enforcement, grant of exception or amendment of bylaws.
6. Consideration of parking problems. (Liability for damage with forceful removal).
7, Consideration of cracking in plaster of units 1 and 3.
8. Election of officers. (Hire bookkeeper, spread and simplify duties of officers).
9. Consideration of Phase IV.
10. New business: P.O. boxes, chimney sweeping, etc.
11. Adjournment.

       Director _____

       Sec-Treas._____

To facilitate preparation for the meeting, it is helpful to include in the notice of the meeting a removable question portion something like the following:

Tear off and return lower portion of page

---

1. Is the date satisfactory? _____
2. Do you plan to attend? _____
3. Place: Ours____ Yours____ Other____
4. Nominee for director:_____
5. Nominee for sec.-treas.:_____

  The meeting will be most successful if the members are comfortable and the surroundings, agreeable: if there is adequate provision for space, seating, tables and proper room temperature.

  The chairman of the meeting, elected from the board, is usually a representative of the developer until nearly all the units of the condominium have been completed. He may be reluctant to act in this capacity, so one of the association members of the board will have to officiate in a more-than-temporary fashion. This can be awkward but quite satisfactory.

  In all meetings, Roberts Rules of Order are followed, somewhat informally and relaxed. Following is a sample of these rules:

Art. I. How Business is Conducted in Deliberative Assemblies.
    1. Introduction of Business
    2. What Precedes Debate
    3. Obtaining the Floor
    4. Motions and Resolutions
    5. Seconding Motions
    6. Stating the Question
    7. Debate
    8. Secondary Motions

    9. Putting the question and announcing the vote
    10. Proper Motions to Use to accomplish Certain Objects

Getting voting bodies for the meeting is often a problem when many owners are out-of-state.

Only unit owners are permitted to vote, one vote per unit. In order to conduct business, the bylaws require a quorum of 50 percent (attendance by half of the unit owners, either in person or by proxy: someone designated by the unit owner to vote in his stead). On the other hand, voting can be done by mail on specific questions, but then the vote to pass a motion must be unanimous, 100 percent.

A proxy is easy to obtain by including in the meeting notice a removable portion such as the following:

Tear off and return lower portion of page

PROXY

To conduct the normal annual business meeting of the River View Condominium Unit Owners Association on _____ 199_,

I appoint_____ to vote as my proxy.

Unit Owner_____

Date   _____

For our condominium the meeting usually spans a period of about two hours.

Finally, minutes of the meeting must be carefully prepared by the secretary, who should have taken adequate notes. It is helpful to mark the agenda as the meeting progresses, thereby insuring conformity and a kind of shorthand notation. The minutes should be typed as soon after the meeting as possible because delay makes recall more difficult and writing slower and more painful. For complete accuracy, the meeting could be recorded on tape.

Appointed Committees

The greatest benefit of committees is to get the unit owners involved in the affairs of their association; this is difficult, and for small condominiums the committees are mostly just temporary. The most important typical committees are Architectural Control, Finance, Membership, Security, Budget, and Nomination.

These advisory groups do not set policy or make rules; that is strictly a function of the board of directors, to whom the committees will only recommend actions.

Committees are useful to ease the load on officers of the association. For example, a committee of one can be appointed any time by the board to investigate some problem or obtain certain information and report back to the board.

Here are some examples of committee work at River View: the appointment of one person to obtain all necessary information for strengthening and repair of the sea wall; two people to prepare signs for controlling the flow of traffic; and several people to investigate and obtain bids for a major re-roofing project.

Board of Directors

This board is the heart of the association. Its job is management as specified by the bylaws: enforcing, making policy, and administering. It controls, but is always subject to recall; and always there is rule by the majority.

River View has five directors, all of whom, other than interim directors appointed by the developer, must be owners or co-owners of units of the condominium. The following diagram shows the position of the directors in the government of the condominium:

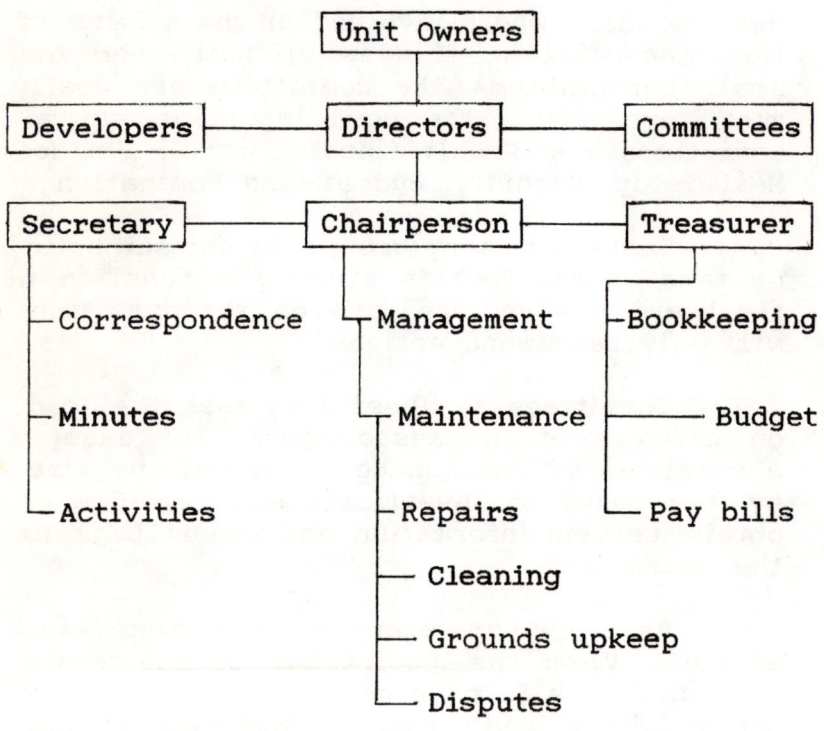

The powers and duties of the board of directors shall include, but not be limited to, the following:

1. Care for association property.
2. Determine and make necessary expenditures.
3. Collect dues from unit owners.
4. Hire and fire needed personnel.
5. Hire legal, accounting, or other personnel required.
6. Open bank accounts and designate signatories.
7. Purchase units of the condominium at judicial sales.
8. Obtain insurance or bonds.
9. Alter association property as needed.
10. Enforce all rules and regulations.
11. Incorporate the association if desired.
12. Make new rules as required, still subject to the will of the unit owners.

In the end, when usual means to secure compliance with the rules are unsuccessful, after all the efforts of meetings, committees and the board have been made, the board can resort to court action.

4

MANAGEMENT

MANAGEMENT

Bookkeeping--Maintaining buildings--Maintaining Grounds--Administering Problems--Collecting Dues--Choosing Type of Management.

Management means handling, controlling, and directing the affairs of the condominium. It means laying out and arranging affairs, conducting or running them, announcing and recording them. The general plan of management is set forth in the bylaws, further refined by the board of directors and even modified by vote of the unit owners.

Management is some kind of bookkeeping, and it is caring for physical properties (maintaining buildings and grounds); it is administering problems of communications, committees, activities, members (including rentals), rules and violations, security and emergencies.

Bookkeeping

The principal items of bookkeeping at River View Condominium are laid out and arranged as follows:

1. Checkbook.
2. Unit Owner Ledger.
3. Analysis Ledger. Accounts are: Maintenance, Garbage and grounds, Utilities, Insurance, Administration, Deferred Maintenance (capital replacement), and miscellaneous (including operating reserve and emergency).
4. Budget.

5. Statement of expenses and income.
6. Dues Apportionment.
7. Balance Sheet.
8. Income Tax (Mar. 15).

Insurance is the most expensive account, consuming a full third of the unit owners dues. It also requires cooperation with the real estate agency to ensure that a new owner pays for insurance one full year in advance to provide money for the payment due each September 13. This Money is refunded upon sale of the unit. The insurance plan also includes consideration of director's liability and bonds or licenses for workers.

Handling the affairs of the condominium includes keeping all funds and securities, along with the making of receipts and payouts of all authorized bills.

Maintaining buildings

Caring for physical properties requires mainly carpentry, painting at three- to five-year intervals, cleaning (windows each year, cobwebs, walls every two years) and equipment repair. Typical work at River View was done as follows for 1988:

Item	Cost
Shingle wing walls	$ 343
Paint car ports	
Paint	559
Labor	2599
Outside light bulbs	70
Storm damage repair	750
Chimney repair	131
Miscellaneous	20
Total	$ 4472

Caring for physical properties goes even beyond maintenance to actually altering the common elements when necessary.

Maintaining grounds

The principal requirements for maintaining grounds at River View are:
1. Water lawn. (Wind wetting buildings is a problem). Set sprinklers after mowing a section, and water extra for shrubs.
2. Prune and spray two or three times a year for insects. Use bait for slugs, ortholene on rhododendrons (no watering or mowing at such times).
3. Weed and feed (fertilize) lawn and shrubs three times per year. Use round-up plus hand weeding.
4. Pick up trash.
5. Mow three times per year in north field. The lawn requires mowing for 11 months of the year.

The costs estimated for grounds in 1989 were $ 112 for supplies, $ 57 for sawdust and $ 35 for signs. The estimate for labor was as follows:

Item	Hours
Two sprayings	8
Two hand weedings	8
Two trimmings	8
Three fertilizings	5
Two pick-ups	1
Three mowings, North Field	6
40 lawn mowings	80
Total	116

Maintaining grounds requires a good gardening plan and a gardener—an individual or a nursery who makes regular trips to the grounds and performs special work at the request of the board of directors.

Administering problems

So many problems would end if only the communication were better. For example, an owner was angry and uncooperative because he thought an outside manager was forcing a rule on him. When he learned that his own board of directors had made the rule after careful deliberation, he became agreeable. Good communication means announcing and reporting on events and meetings, preparing effective minutes, keeping good records readily available, and talking to each other.

Whenever a problem requires research, a contracting effort or a long time to completion, a committee should probably be appointed to look into it—a committee that provides expertise and eases the load on the directors.

Activities of a small condominium are fewer in number, so have fewer problems. However, even only one activity, transportation, for example, needs to be managed with regard to parking, noise level, kinds of vehicles and number.

Overcoming problems of members, or unit owners, is certainly helped by good communication, but management will do well to be continually on the alert for ways to promote good will. If the difficulty is between owners, they should resolve it themselves—if they can't, management should. And when it does, management will be supported and indemnified by the association. Often the difficulty is with an owner's renter or rental agreement.

Rules and violations are a pressing concern for the administration. Everyone agrees to conform with the bylaws, but the question is how strictly and how quickly.

Since some people think the bylaws can be used more as guidelines than as rigid rules of conduct, administering is difficult. Everything one does in this close communal living affects his neighbor, and what to do about it can be vexatious.

Finally, in the matter of security and emergencies, our own problems have been minor, although their potential for worse is considerable. There has been no case of breaking and entering, and the only emergency has been to stop rain leaks from storm damage; and this, in a period of ten years. Even so, thought is given to fencing and gates for security--to better locks and lighting for even more security. And a plan is always needed for quick entry to units when the owner is away for long periods of time; keys to units should be stored safely and in an orderly manner.

Collecting Dues

When a unit owner causes the problem of being late in payment of dues, the simplest solution is to mail one or more letters typically as follows:

LETTERS
for
DELINQUENT DUES

The following four letters are to be sent in order, so that anyone who is late in paying dues will be induced to pay them on time.

FIRST LETTER--SEND AFTER 15 DAYS LATE (Now in default)

                                River View Condominium
                                Unit Owners Assn.
                                P.O. Box _____
                                _____, OR 97439
                                _____, 199_

Name
Address

_____
_____

Dear Unit Owner:

We note that your dues account is overdue and that you owe the following sum through _____, 199_.

Knowing that you may have overlooked this matter, or had other problems, we are sending this letter to remind you that accounts are due on the first of the month.

If we can help in any way, please call or write the secretary-treasurer.

                Sincerely,

SECOND LETTER--SEND 15 DAYS AFTER THE FIRST LETTER
                (30 days after due date)

                                River View Condominium
                                Unit Owners Assn.
                                P.O. Box _____
                                _____, OR 97439
                                _____,199_

Name
Address

_____

_____

Dear Unit Owner:

On _____, 199_, we sent you a letter concerning your overdue payment of dues totaling $_____. Despite that reminder, we have received no payment nor explanation for its omission since that time.

The Board of Directors will not allow lateness in payments by anyone, because that would be costly and unfair to the other unit owners; and, as you well know, entirely unacceptable in business. Accordingly, if payment is not received within fifteen days from the date of this letter, your account will be considered by the Board.

Incidentally, it should be noted that, according to our bylaws, any attorney fees in this matter will be charged to the delinquent.

Hopefully, this procedure will not be required.

                          Sincerely,

THIRD LETTER--SEND 15 DAYS AFTER SECOND LETTER
            (Send after telephone call)

                          River View Condominium
                          Unit Owners Assn.
                          P.O. Box _____
                          _____, OR 97439
                          _____,199_

Name
Address ___

_____
_____

Dear Unit Owner:

We have written two letters to you requesting payment of your delinquent dues account.

Since we have not heard from you for an entire month, we are sorry to say that collection of the fees must be turned over to the Association's attorney.

        Sincerely,

        Director

        Ordered by the Board
        of Directors

cc: (Mortgage Company)

FOURTH LETTER--SEND PROMPTLY AFTER THE THIRD
   (From the Association Attorney)

        River View Condominium
        Unit Owners Assn.
        P.O. Box _____
        _____, OR 97439
        _____,199_

Name
Address

_____
_____

Dear Unit Owner:

I have your account from River View Condominium showing that you owe _____ for dues. Enclosed is a copy of their ledger showing that debt and your recent payment re-record. Your last payment was made in _____ of 19__. As you can see, this is the _____ time your account has been in arrears.

These dues are necessary to pay for insurance, maintenance, utilities, garbage collection, replacements and administration. Your failure to pay the dues on time is costly and unfair to the other unit owners.

Consequently, this letter orders that you pay at once the _____ owed and that you pay all future assessments on time.

To do this I suggest you authorize your rental manager to withhold rent until your debt is paid in full. Furthermore, I suggest you authorize him to continue to pay dues monthly from the rent received.

As a result, you would receive from your manager the balance of your rent, and the Association would know they are receiving their fees on time.

If you do not pay the balance of _____ and devise a procedure for timely payments, the Board will have to initiate further action. This would be either a suit against you to obtain judgment and to execute on rent payments or it would be foreclosure of the unit and sale to pay off your debt.

I think you will agree from the enclosure shown that your payment system has been at fault and that you need to correct it; therefore, please give it your immediate attention. If I do not hear from you or the Association does not receive its dues by _____

1st, we will initiate the legal moves needed to obtain payment.

Yours very truly,

_____

_____

Enclosure

cc: _____, Director

Choosing kinds of management

Four kinds are suggested: self management, professional management, partial outside management, or a combination of these. Self management is the choice for condominiums with up to about 20 units. Being small they simply can't afford to hire managers—the board does all the managing, without recompense, as we do at River View. If someone on the board is a handyman or jack of all trades, work can be planned more economically, although some requires licensing. Usually, the work will be part doing-it-yourself and part hiring help.

Professional management is desirable but expensive, and it is very scarce in this relatively new industry. There are no requirements yet, no licenses. A manager needs some bookkeeping capability, a concernment for maintenance, some manual labor skill, and perhaps a background in motel management. This type is able to remain aloof from the owners, to resist meddling and to be fair and impartial.

Many real estate agencies advertise property management and can provide partial service from outside in a manner similar to that of a professional manager. Often this may be only a bookkeeping service. But even when it is much more, it is not as complete and well suited as self management. A good situation results when the agency has a bookkeeper, a licensed handyman, and a long list of contractors in all the needed disciplines.

A combination of the foregoing types of management can be arranged for larger condominiums, where the manager is hired to work directly under the chairman of the board of directors, and several other employees would work for him part time or in shifts. A bookkeeper would be hired to work under the treasurer of the board, perhaps also assisted with part-time help. This arrangement can work well, but not as smoothly as well-organized professional management.

In the end, the board of directors itself will decide how to handle, control and direct the affairs of the condominium--always under the watchful eyes of the association of unit owners.

5

INSURANCE

INSURANCE

Oregon Revised Statutes (ORS)--Bylaws--Experience at River View Condominium--Insurance Summary.

The board of directors must obtain full insurance, consisting of both casualty and liability, to cover the property and people of the condominium. The board is the trustee for the unit owners and is guided in this matter by the requirements spelled out in the controlling rules and regulations, first by the state and second by the bylaws of the association. These will be presented in the following pages.

Oregon Revised Statutes (ORS)

"94.177 Insurance for units and common elements. (1) If the bylaws provide that the association of unit owners has the sole authority to decide whether to repair or reconstruct a unit that has suffered damage or that a unit must be repaired or reconstructed, the board of directors shall obtain and maintain at all times and shall pay for out of the common expense funds, the following insurance covering both the common elements and individual units:

"(a) Property insurance including, but not limited to, fire, extended coverage, vandalism and malicious mischief; and

"(b) Insurance covering the legal liability of the association of unit owners, the unit owners individually and the manager, including but not limited to the board of directors, the public and the unit owners and their invitees or tenants, incident to ownership, supervision, control or use of the property. There may be excluded from the policy required under this paragraph, coverage of a unit owner, other than coverage as a member of the association of unit owners or board of directors, for liability arising out of acts or omissions of that unit owner and liability incident to the ownership or use of the part of the property as to which that unit owner has the exclusive use or occupancy. Liability insurance required under this paragraph shall be issued on a comprehensive liability basis and shall provide a cross liability indorsement providing that the rights of a named insured under the policy shall not prejudice any action against another named insured."

Bylaws

"17. Insurance. The board of directors shall obtain such liability insurance as the board deems necessary to protect the association, its officers or employees, and the unit owners. In addition, the board of directors, as trustee for the unit owners, shall obtain such casualty insurance as necessary to protect the entire condominium property. The board of directors, in its discretion, may obtain such other insurance as it deems necessary to protect the interests of the association or unit owners. The board of directors shall conduct an annual insurance review which shall include an appraisal of all improvements contained in the condominium. No unit owner may engage in any activity which might jeopardize the insurance coverage described herein. Insurance policies obtained hereunder shall be master policies insuring the association, its officers and directors, the manager or managing agent, if any, and all unit owners and their mortgagees, as their respective interests may appear, and shall include the following provisions, if possible:

"(a) Casualty coverage shall include those risks covered by a standard fire insurance policy with extended coverage endorsement and shall be for the full replacement cost without deduction of depreciation.

"(b) Such policy shall contain a waiver of the usual proration clause, elimination of the usual 'no other insurance' provision, and waiver of any right of subrogation as against any coinsured.

"(c) Such policy shall require the insurance company to give notice of cancellation to the insureds and any mortgagees covered by loss payable clauses.

"(d) Such policy shall bear a mortgagee's clause or a loss-payable clause in favor of any mortgagee or lender requesting the same, but such clause shall not give the mortgagee or lender the right to preempt payment of the insurance proceeds to the association or to control whether or not the damage is repaired. The insurer shall likewise waive its right to determine whether the damage should be repaired, and loss adjustment and control of the proceeds of the policy shall rest in the association as trustee for the unit owners.

"(e) Liability coverage should cover any unit owner for his acts or omissions in connection with the condominium and cover any liability arising out of ownership of any unit of the condominium, and should contain a severability of interests provision so as to cover one unit owner for his liability to another unit owner.

"15. Liability and Indemnification of Directors, Manager or Managing Agent. The directors shall not be liable to the association for any mistake of judgment, negligence, or otherwise except for their own willful misconduct or bad faith. The asssociation shall indemnify and hold harmless each director and the manager or managing agent, if any, against all contractual liability to others arising out of contracts made by the board of directors, manager or managing agent on behalf of the asociation unless any such contract shall have been made in bad faith or contrary to the provisions of the declaration or of these bylaws. Each director and the manager or managing agent, if any, shall be indemnified by the association against all expenses and liabilities, including attorneys' fees, reasonably incurred or imposed upon them in connection with any proceeding to which they may be a party, or which they may become involved, by reason of being or having been a director, manager or managing agent and shall be indemnified upon any reasonable settlement thereof; provided, however, there shall be no indemnity if the director, manager or managing agent is adjudged guilty of willful nonfeasance, misfeasance or malfeasance in the performance of his or her duties."

Experience at River View Condominium

In the beginning, insurance was provided by the developer. Then the association selected its own insurance company; and finally that company was exchanged for one nearby that had a good rating and tested well against other companies.

We had liability coverage on one hand, and on the other, instead of all-risk, named peril coverage; including fire, lightning, wind, hail, limited explosion, smoke, auto, airplane, riot and vandalism and the bad one: water, either by storms, plumbing failures, freezing pipes or floods.

Our chosen company provides individual unit owner's insurance, in addition to the common area insurance, and unit or skin insurance. There is a policy available at $20,000 per unit for personal property, cabinets, carpets and paint.

Being on an estuary, we are subject to flooding at rare intervals, so flood insurance has always been an important consideration. Only 25 years ago a devastating tidal wave inundated the area; should it recur it would cover our lower floors to a depth of several feet.

Insurance Summary

The following is a brief summary of in-insurance at River View on January 26, 1989:

>RIVER VIEW CONDOMINIUM
>UNIT OWNERS ASSOCIATION
>
>Insurance Summary
>9-13-88 to 9-13-89

PROPERTY:
- A. Limits: Blanket buildings and contents for $1,350,000 (Phase I building for $ 750,000 and $ 6,000 contents; Phase II building for $ 350,000; Phase III building for $ 250,000).

- B. Coverage: Special form perils with the primary exclusions being flood, earthquake, wear and tear, etc. A 90% coinsurance clause applies.

C. Deductible: A $ 100 deductible applies to each loss.

LIABILITY:
A. Limit: $ 1,000,000 combined single limit for bodily injury and property damage; $ 5,000 medical payments per person/$ 25,000 per accident.

B. Covers: Premises, operations, personal injury (libel, slander, defamation of character, wrongful entry /eviction, etc.), non-owned auto liability and products coverage if any.

ANNUAL PREMIUM: $ 5,109.00

OPTIONS:
A. Increase property values.
B. Increase property deductible.
C. Umbrella − $ 1,000,000 or $ 2,000,000.
D. Directors E & O coverage.

NATIONAL FLOOD INSURANCE PROGRAM

6

PROBLEMS

PROBLEMS

Restitutions--Finances--Bylaws--Common Utilities--Construction--Unit Numbering--Dues--Garbage and Grounds--Leaks--Lateness Penalty--Marina--Meetings--Maintenance--Deferred Maintenance--Roofing Repair--Sea Wall--Arguments--Need for Legal Help--Rentals--Absenteeism--Emergencies--Communication--Security.

People everywhere have little problems in day-to-day living and trying to get along with each other. An excellent system, such as a condominium, has them too. In fact, due to the closer relationships, some problems may become severe.

People need to be satisfied at every step along the way, planning, constructing, correcting faults, maintaining, managing, protecting, buying and renting. Lack of agreement can require legal help, even for small associations.

These problems are part of the picture of condominium living, so we will run through them in the following pages, as experienced at River View and other Condominiums.

Restitutions

Damages, construction faults, injuries, and other issues occur continuously in daily life, but restitution for them may be difficult, on the one hand, because the association of unit owners wants to get the greatest possible contribution from the builder-developer --on the other hand, because the latter wants to contribute as little as possible, keeping expenses down and making a profit; still, he will try to maintain good will and keep the premises as attractive as possible in order to promote sales.

Sometimes a third party can make these restitutions, as in the case of storm damage where the insurance company pays the bill, or as in the case of a wall failure near a public street where the city will pay.

Finances

The money matters of a condominium un-undoubtedly present troublesome problems. Nevertheless, at River View the solution developed gradually over the years from a good start in the bylaws. In the beginning, the contractor's wife managed finances for the developer, receiving pay at 10 percent of the total expenses. Almost at once it became apparent that a detailed yearly budget would have to be prepared. And this proved to be a continuing prime subject of discussion.

Also, a statement of expenses and income was an important financial report that would have to be prepared each year.

Eventually, six accounts would be established to handle most financial transactions. Some items do not fit easily into these categories, and it may be hard to decide who is responsible for an item. For example, outside lighting and grounds upkeep could well be the responsibility of the unit owners, but a trailer park and an office on condominium land is the responsibility of the developer. On the other hand, the marina, the lease for which is held by the association of unit owners, and the docks, owned by the developer, are the responsibility of both.

This part-time work at River View soon became too onorous for the contractor's wife, who resigned, and one of the unit owners took over the books. This owner, as secretary-treasurer, handled five accounts and shifted monies among them at the end of the year to keep them solvent. Two of them went into the red the first year because of increasing costs for water and sewage disposal. But the condominium was growing. In 1983, income and expense balanced at $6,000. The next year, income was up to $7,845.

A very difficult issue was to get someone to serve as secretary-treasurer, especially since it was evident that soon someone would have to be hired as part-time bookkeeper. Nevertheless, the secretary-treasurer was mollified by payment at eight percent of monthly expenses and help from two directors, who would try to phase in a working manager (bookkeeper-coordinator). But, as the bank balance grew there was interest, and that caused income tax to rear its ugly head. Still, the tax form was simple and a director filled it out.

After seven years, with 17 units, the eight percent manager's fee had risen to $1,049 (Annual expenditure was $13,112.). It was discovered that to simplify the books all bills should be paid as near to the due date as possible. And the $500 remains of a temporary legal account would have to be returned to the unit owners.

Bylaws

Through the years the unit owners have done a good job in observing the bylaws and avoiding problems with them. However, at times the owners must be reminded that no dogs or cats should be running around loose outdoors. At such times the animals must be on leashes. At one time, it was recommended that renters be given copies of the bylaws.

Another reminder was to park the car only in its own numbered space. Then, of course, there is the reminder cautioning against making any loud noise, especially after 10 p.m. Once someone dared to fire a canon!

Recently, people were parking in such a manner as to prevent an owner from backing her car, and the result was the installation of a "no-parking" sign.

Common Utilities

Electric bills are metered individually by units, but all outside lighting has a single meter, as a common utility like water and sewage. This has confused the owners, so they had to be reminded to pay their bills directly to the electric company.

Payment for the outside lighting has been a vexing problem because the developer at first had the lighting all to himself in the trailer park; then it was extended to our new units, and we shared in the cost; but now the developer says he will no longer pay any of the cost because the trailer park has been removed and lighting is practically all for the benefit of the units.

Construction

Delays of all kinds plague construction. Building our condominium has taken a long time mainly because the market had weakened; the developer points out that he is waiting for the demand for condominiums to pick up. It was five years after completion of the first eight-unit building when he announced he would begin construction of the remaining units of the project, but they were to be only 4-plex, instead of 8-plex--The beautiful models and plans went down the drain. In fact, there is no guarantee against the ultimate delay: failure to complete the project.

Paper work adds to the problems of construction. For example, the second building (Phase 2) required the recording of a supplemental declaration on April 25, 1984. Therefore, that is the date when Phase 2 became a part of River View Condominium, and 4-1-84 was the agreed-upon date with the developer to begin charging monthly dues for Phase 2. It should be noted, however, that this supplement is not a simple matter, because it also requires the preparation of amendments both to the declaration and to the bylaws.

Another problem is selling the units to get the money to build more. At one time, two units in Phase 1 and three in Phase 2 were for sale.

It wasn't until 1988, after a bitter court settlement, that the latest phase was selling and the developer could proceed with construction. His latest plans included the three last phases of the project--four-unit buildings. Since the best selling feature of the phases is the view, he provided one phase with a good view to the southwest, one, to the southeast, and the third, to the south between phases 1 and 2.

All of this activity is part of the excitement of condominium living: the additions of new units and their sale, the resale of other units and the comings and goings of such close neighbors.

Unit Numbering

One potentially bothersome problem with condominiums is the numbering of units. If great care is not taken when numbers are assigned, a tangle can result--like the one we have at River View. This is a common problem, exhibited to some degree in the streets of almost every city. Where is the city with consistent street and house numbering?

Our first building (Phase I) was assigned letter-numerals, (e.g., B-2), with odd numbers on lower units and even on upper because the ninth unit, the office, had to be odd and lower. Then Phase II was given only numbers, even below, odd above. Some uniformity was achieved by dropping letters from Phase I, but the numbers were still in reverse order.

Phase III came in with mixed numbers, even-odd below and above. Phase IV did the same--except that the order went from west to east, instead of from east to west.

How could the numbering system be worse? You can't deal with a unit if you can't identify it. Bookkeeping was in dire straights, and many other important services were having identification troubles: Emergency vehicles, such as fire and police, were having trouble locating units in difficulty; City Hall was mixing water and sewer bills; the Post Office was confused with mail; the PUD was having similar difficulty with power bills; our real estate and rental companies were moderately confused by the unit numbers; even the insurance company was complaining about its problems in bookkeeping and billing, and was wanting any reasonable, uniform system. It was the developer, collaborating with the realtor, who had indifferently set up the present system.

Most unit owners agreed that a change should be made, but each had a favorite system and couldn't agree to adopt another. Furthermore, any changes in numbering would have to be run through the state statutes and the declaration.

In conclusion, since the unit owners like the numbers under which they bought their units, it has been agreed that no changes will be made to existing numbering. However, all new phases coming in will have numbers similar to those of the last phase, clearly and boldly labeled.

Dues

Some people at River View objected to paying dues on the basis of square footage. It didn't seem fair to pay more for lawn care just because you had a large living room. On the other hand, it is obvious that a large floor means a large roof, and care for that does require more payment. It was shown that a dues formula based midway between square footage and equal sharing would be more equitable, and that was agreeable to owners of large units. However, some owners of small units objected to such a change. As a result, since the rules on this matter required 100 percent approval of the owners, the revision of the dues formula could not be made.

Some condominiums do have equal sharing of dues, and there the owners of small units object: they should not have to pay as much for upkeep as the owner of a large unit.

Garbage and Grounds

The garbage part of this has been simple--mostly a reminder to people to put garbage in the bin only. Of course, on busy weekends extra pickups sometimes had to be ordered. Then, as more units were added to the condominium, the number of pickups had to be increased.

The grounds part is not so simple. At first the individual owners like to mow the lawn, but soon a gardener has to be hired and given a key to the storage room.

Next comes the weeding, spreading bark mulch and spraying for both weeds and insects; but now the environmentalists object, and tell us that we may harm the environment only to the extent absolutely necessary to save the grounds.

Whoever does the watering thinks about the great amount of time that must be spent. Sooner or later, the suggestion for a sprinkling system comes up, as it did with us and was tabled a number of times. When it was tabled the last time, the reason was that final landscaping plans had not yet been developed. Now, a system has been installed.

Leaks

If you happen to live in an area subject to severe wind and rain storms, sooner or later you probably will have trouble with leaks into your unit. In our case the first leak came from water ponding on the skylight over the stairway, seeping through the putty seal and staining the ceiling. Another skylight had insufficient overlap of flashings and water blew through into the bathroom. Still another, clouded up with water between the double panes. Incidentally, flashings have been at fault in many places: around chimneys, at vent pipes, near air vents and in roof valleys.

We had an extensive problem with leaks when shingles were blown from the roof.

An unexpected leak developed when a plastic wall vent lost its hood after a period of decay and cracking, and water blew into the shingle wall, seeped along a beam to an opening and stained the living room wall.

When water ponded inside a chimney pipe, even without rain, it had to be the result of condensation in a unit long vacant. However, when a chimney leak occurred, even with perfect roof construction, it was traced to an outside shingle wall without building paper under the shingles.

Once, when ice and snow had accumulated on the roof, rain ponded on the ice, backed up under the shingles and dripped to the floors of several units. Fortunately, a neighbor set out pots to catch the dripping water. Incidentally, it is a good idea to make frequent inspections of units whose owners are long away.

In all of this, who should make the repairs? The developer? The association? The unit owner? Or the insurance company? And which part should he do? The carpentry, the plastering, or the painting?

Lateness Penalty

Here is a vexing problem: how to reform the someone who won't pay dues on time. Most condominiums allow for this by imposing an interest rate penalty, and ours is one of them. However, nine percent interest per annum is hardly enough to force payment. We thought a more severe penalty was required, such as a flat $10 every time a payment became overdue. This seemed a good idea until we found that our bylaws required a 75 percent vote of the unit owners in order to make changes in financial matters. Nevertheless, in some future meeting we may still be able to muster enough votes to effect this desirable amendment.

Marina

When the developer purchased the land for our condominium, it included an old marina consisting of some 100 decrepit boat slips. Probably the greatest value of the marina was as a sales inducement; each purchaser of a unit was given the free use of a boat slip, and when the condominium would finally be completed the marina would become the property of the unit owners association. Included with the marina would be the lease right to the underlying land. In the beginning, this seemed like a good idea, but little did anyone then know what a headache it was to become.

Our doubts were raised when the developer paid $ 22,300 for dredging sand that would soon wash back with the swift currents of the tide. Doubts were raised further when he estimated that repair of the rotting slips would cost another $ 10,000. Add to that the operating costs and the ever-rising rental cost of the lease. Then bear in mind that, should the developer decide for some reason to declare his project finished, he could immediately unload the marina onto an association of only nine unit owners.

In fear, we consulted an attorney, agreed to a longer construction time and won from the developer the promise that the project would not be called complete until at least 33 units had been sold.

Soon the developer found that the marina was costing him too much, and the full project of 66 units was too ambitious, so he sold the half which contained the marina. Of course, the marina lease and boat slips were still understood to be available to the then-existing unit owners, but they had not signed an agreement to that effect, and the association had not been consulted. Now, attorneys were consulted by all three participants, the new buyer, the developer and the asssociation.

The unit owners were asking for guarantees of the following conditions: View preservation, reasonable upkeep, security, high-class construction, completion, buffer zones, good lighting, and noise isolation. In addition, the owners wanted the thirteen original units to have priority for boat slips at 50 percent fee reduction. They believed that the marina could be profitable to the association and could provide leverage over the developer in future dealings. In return for all of this, they would be willing to give up all rights to the marina and submerged land.

In the end, the gains for the unit owners were questionable, and the cost for legal fees was considerable for each owner.

Meetings

The main problem with meetings is picking a time when most can attend.

Letters to and minutes of the Association of Unit Owners of River View and their board of directors are available; and for your interest, the dates, attendance and brief notes of the meetings are presented as follows:

1. 9/6/81. Association. Six present, plus two realtors. First organizational meeting.
2. 10/29/81. Board. Five. Elected chairman.
3. 8/15/82. Association. Five.
4. 9/29/82. Board. Four and one proxy.
5. 4/28/83. Board. To increase dues and amend bylaws.
6. 7/5/83. Association. To prepare for annual meeting.
7. 8/20/83. Association. Ten.
8. 9/11/83. Board. Seven.
9. 10/8/83. Association. Ten. Special meeting.
10. 10/17/83. Letter. Amendments and costs of marina.
11. 5/20/84. Letter. Notice of July annual meeting.
12. 7/14/84. Association. Fourteen.
13. 8/10/85. Association. Five. No quorum, so no official business.
14. 6/21/86. Association. Fourteen.
15. 8/8/87. Association. Twelve.
16. 11/7/87. Association. Eight. Special meeting.
17. 4/20/88. Letter. Plan July annual meeting.
18. 8/16/88. Association. Four plus six proxies. Barely a quorum.
19. 8/10/88. Association. Six plus

five proxies and two guests. Quorum was 59.05 percent. Reconvened.
20. 7/15/89. Association.

Maintenance

The yearly maintenance work is merely a matter of many small jobs; the question is how to accomplish them timely and economically. Some jobs result from suggestions or complaints of unit owners: Was the carpenter paid too much for wall repair? For this question, the unit owner had to be reminded to present his complaint to a director, not directly to the repair man. When the developer's park manager also serviced our grounds, the bookkeeping had to show careful separation of costs.

In time, birds began nesting in the carport, covering our cars with excrement. This problem was solved by nailing slanted boards between rafters over the level nesting areas.

Light bulbs continually burn out and need replacement soon, requiring frequent night inspections. Some fixtures are of a design that is hard to replace and require expensive bulbs.

Painting is one of the larger jobs because some part of the condominium needs to be done every year. One time it is the garbage bin; another, the railings, and still another, the fast-weathering south walls. And, of course, the actual painting is often not as big a job as the preliminary caulking, sealing, scraping, repairing and washing. On the other hand, interior walls are not common area--painting them is strictly up to the individual owner, lessening the load on the management team.

Other maintenance jobs include window washing, repairing posts struck by someone's car, replacing frozen hose bibs and inspecting and cleaning chimneys and wall vents. Although windows are not common elements, the association has voted that management should do the washing--it is easier.

When part of the building settles and cracks develop, all the units involved must be examined; responsibility is determined and payment is requested from either the insurance company, the developer, the association, the individual owners involved or a combination of these.

Sometimes major construction by the association is necessary, as when building paper has been omitted under wall shingles for chimneys, causing severe water leaks in units below. If the expense for this might exceed $2500, the directors must obtain permission by vote of the association to spend the additional amount.

Obviously, our developer made many mistakes due to lack of experience in this area before he began construction. However, now at last he builds new additions with excellence. He should have read this book before he started back in 1978.

Deferred Maintenance

Soon one recognizes that annual maintenance will not accomplish all the maintenance required. Money must also be provided for long-term items such as a worn or damaged roof or collapsed swimming pool. To provide for this problem at River View, a deferred maintenance account was established at 10 cents per square foot of building area, effective

Sept. 1, 1984. At the same time an operating reserve account was established to provide money for emergencies when regular accounts might be temporarily depleted.

The roof at River View failed before the deferred maintenance account had increased sufficiently to pay for a new roof. Payment was accomplished by a combination of special assessments and contributions from the developer, whose construction method had been inadequate--i.e., he had used staples in place of sturdy shingle nails.

Roofing Repair

On a storm-tossed coast, such as ours, roof damage, sooner or later, is almost assured. But the problem is more than just the force of the storm: Salt in the air and water is very corrosive and took only four years to sever completely the staples holding the shingles. Because he clearly had used a poor construction method (using staples), the developer agreed to pay two-thirds of the cost of a new roof, leaving the remainder to us.

However, the second building, which had only a two-year-old roof, and also had to be re-roofed, was another matter. The developer had tired of the continuing calls for repairs and said he would pay the two-thirds only if we would release him from any future claims on the roof.

At one place, the removal of ventilators caused the roof to sweat, so that the vents required replacement.

Of course, the storms damaged more than just shingles: They ripped off skylights and blew water under flashings and shingles; they tore off chimney caps and dropped trees on sheds.

Sea Wall

Our condominium has only 12 feet of lawn between it and the broad estuary, which has a ten-foot tide and wicked waves. Accordingly, the rock wall, or bulkhead, lining the bank is very important. When small rocks washed out and thin areas were noted, we had to decide between adding more crumbly rock or going to concrete. Fortunately, we found leftovers of hard rock from the jetties, and soon placed a good lining, having a deep toe trench. But the unit owners suffered a cost of $7,130.

Still, our problems are not over, because construction of additional buildings has required extension of our bulkhead, and we must ride herd to asure a quality of construction that matches it. Furthermore, similar assurance must be obtained from our upstream neighbor, who is constructing a waterfront project.

Arguments

Arguments between neighbors sometimes become a major problem in a condominium. For example, someone might make a loud noise at night at the wall adjoining his neighbor, who complains bitterly, and the fight is on. Or, someone parks in his neighbor's space, albeit temporarily, and again a fight ensues.

Perhaps the best way to describe the problem is to present action in such cases by the board of directors of our condominium as follows. First, a letter from the board:

"Dear Unit Owner:

"The directors of the unit owners association held a meeting on Sept 21 to discuss violations of the bylaws.

"People have been parking behind cars of unit owners, blocking egress, sometimes critically in hospital emergencies. The bylaws state: 'The use of the common elements (pavement) shall not be obstructed by any unit owner.' Accordingly, a 'NO PARKING' sign will be posted. A clearly visible sign is necessary in order to have a car towed away at the owner's expense. However, the object is to prevent outsiders from parking in such places, not to tow them away.

"Boat trailers in carports will have to be removed. The bylaws state:'Except with the consent of the board of directors, no boat or boat trailer shall be parked on any portion of the condominium.'

"A car may not be left in a parking space for days at a time. The bylaws state: 'No parking area shall be used as a parking place for motor vehicles not in regular family use and good operating condition.'

"With regard to guest parking, Phase I has only two outside spaces at the east and west ends of the building, which should be reserved for guests only. Phase II has two spaces for each owner, one being for his guest. Phase III has one parking space for each owner and, again, only the two outside spaces for all guests. All other guests will have to park in the field or on the streets.

"Antennas, also, will have to be removed from the outside of the buildings. The bylaws state: 'No unit owner may install a television antenna or radio antenna on the exterior of a unit except as authorized in writing by the board of directors.'

"Unit owners are cautioned not to permit loud noises in their units, such as the slamming of doors. The bylaws state: 'No noxious or offensive activities shall be carried on in any unit, nor shall anything be done which is a source of annoyance to residents.'

"The foregoing requirements may seem harsh to some, but surely the bylaws are intended to be followed for the general good of the unit owners. Accordingly, please see that the requirements are met."

Sincerely,

Director

Then, a ballot proposal:

"BALLOT (11/21/88)
"This is an emergency meeting of the board of directors, conducted by telephone in accordance with the bylaws. (Much discussion has taken place by telephone and among directors). The subject is Article VII, Section 6g of the bylaws: 'Except with the consent of the board of directors of the association or the manager, no travel trailer, boat or boat trailer, or other recreational vehicles, other motor homes and campers installed on trucks, shall be parked on any portion of the condominium.'
"A unit owner in Phase II, with two parking spaces (only Phase II has this), has used one for his boat trailer for several years. He has now been informed that this violates the bylaws and he should remove the trailer, but he refuses.
"The board appears to have the following four choices:
    1. Enforce the rule.
    2. Give consent to this parking as
       a special case.
    3. Revise the bylaws.
    4. Give consent until the association

can vote at it's next annual meeting.

Signature_____

"Please indicate your vote by circling the number of your choice and sign your name.

"Another ballot will be sent so you can vote on the winner of these choices."

Need for Legal Help

It appears that no matter how small the condominium is it will require the services of an attorney. We had to have them twice already in dealings with our developer and with other buyers. You might wonder if the services are worth the cost; they are if they are necessary, but if you can possibly avoid them, you should. Sometimes, you only need advice.

In a system larger than ours in the same town, an attorney had to be engaged not only for updating bylaws but also for placing and closing liens against owners who were late in paying assessments or who even refused to make the payments.

Rentals

Renting at River View presents few problems because demand for accommodations is high. Even now we are searching for an available unit for a nearby businessman. Nevertheless, these choice units command high prices that make them unaffordable to many. Consequently, the people who rent them can afford to show more interest in taking care of the property.

Forth-five percent of our residents are unit owners, and the remainder are renters. Therefore, they do not usually care as much for the property as they would were all of them owners.

One problem with having so many renters is that we don't have enough unit owners readily available to serve on the board and help in the management and operation of the condominium.

Another problem is renter turnover. We require that rentals endure for at least 30 days. A nearby condominium, renting daily, needs more staff and lacks the friendly atmosphere of neighborliness.

Rentals are managed by outside real estate companies or unit owners even though they might be managed more efficiently by the association. It just doesn't have the personnel for that much more management.

Generally, it would be unthinkable not to have rentals, because they are a comforting inducement to prospective buyers.

Absenteeism

The problem of unit owners being away from their units deserves some attention. As noted above, quick action may not be possible during an emergency such as fire, storm or flood when the owner is not there for advice or entry through a locked door.

Conditions are even worse when a renter is away, because he or she, caring much less about the upkeep of the unit and premises, provides less for problems.

Even a renter is more helpful than nobody in a unit, but still the absence of the owner is felt when a body is needed to serve on a committee or to vote in a meeting. At best, the board must take time and trouble to secure a proxy for the owner's vote.

In summary, when units are to be sold, it pays to make special efforts to secure local buyers who will live in their units and will want to take good care of their investment. It is an easy temptation to the developer to sell to a rich prospect from out of state, but this temptation should be resisted to the last while searching for a local prospect.

Emergencies

When they plan to be away, before they leave the units, the owners can be helpful for emergencies. They could be close with their neighbors, perhaps even leaving them keys to the units. They could leave with the secretary such information as the location of the shut-off valve for the water, the location of the electric service panel and even their own health records. Incidentally, it is good to have someone who lives at the condominium to be trained in first aid.

Unit owners could well be reminded that someone might have to set out pots to catch dripping water during a severe storm, shut off water during a freeze, warn of a fire or a flood and close openings.

To avoid fire emergencies, smoke detectors are a must, and they need to be inspected frequently.

Communication

Information of many kinds is important to satisfactory condominium living: Special effort should be made by the board to inform unit owners about what is going on. Much can be said in just plain talking face to face; even more, by telelphone; and still more, in careful detail, by mail. An informed association is happier and better functioning.

Eventually, as the association grows in size, a monthly newsletter becomes a feasible and harmonius means to inform the members. It can report on sales, rentals, construction, changes, meetings, activities and entertainments.

Finally, we should consider the problem of complaints and suggestions. No matter where it is or how big it is the condominium will experience complaints. And it is best that unit owners and renters understand that they should bring their troubles only to the board of directors or officers, not to employees or other owners. The officers should then resolve the matter as soon as possible in as friendly a manner as possible. Often the problem can be settled by an officer, but sometimes it requires a meeting of the association.

Security

Even condominiums have the problem of guarding against intruders. And for this, good lighting at night is the primary protection; increase it with clear bulbs, top reflectors and light-reflecting walls. A security guard and patroling are not justified until the condominium has grown much larger, and even then it is more economical to begin with part-time help from unit owners. A number of aids to security are mentioned in the following paragraphs.

When you are to be away from home, don't say or leave indications that you may be away.

Visitors to any recreation facilities should wear identification tags.

Deadbolts should be installed on all unit doors.

Keys should not be given out indiscriminately, even to contractors. They should be given to the manager or an officer in case of emergency.

Also when you are away, try to give the appearance that your unit is occupied. You can do this by not allowing newspapers to collect, by putting timers on a lamp or television set to turn it on at the usual time and by arranging for usual lawn care. A car parked in your driveway or space would help.

Finally, inform the neighbors that you will be away, and make it easy for them to watch your place by leaving lights on and trimming shrubbery that obstructs their view. You might even inform the police to be on the lookout.

7
BOOKKEEPING

BOOKKEEPING

Checkbook--Unit Owner Ledger--Analysis Ledger
--Budget--Statement of Expenses and Income--
Dues Apportionment Statement--Balance Sheet--
Income Tax

The bookkeeping plan for our small condominium is so simple that it does not require a computer, only a calculator.

Three books are used: 1. Checkbook. 2. Unit Owner Ledger. 3. Analysis Ledger. Four additional sheets are necessary at year end: Budget, Statement of Expenses and Income, Dues Apportionment Statement and Balance Sheet.

Before running through the descriptions of these books, let us go through the simple procedure required at the end of each month.

Since we use the cash method, all necessary figures are found in the checkbook, the primary one being the cash balance, which is determined by finding the balance figure that is reconciled with the bank statement and adding to it only amounts that may intervene before the end of the month.

From the checkbook, only entrees for unit owners are entered in the unit owner ledger; but all entrees in the checkbook are entered in the analysis ledger, completing the routine work. Later, come the interesting jobs: the budget and the statement of expenses and income.

Checkbook

Little need be said about this book because it is standard and very common. However, since it is the source of all bookkeeping items, it is very important, and great care should be exercised in writing figures correctly and making everything clear.

1990		RECORD ALL CHARGES OR CREDITS THAT AFFECT YOUR ACCOUNT					BALANCE	
NUMBER	DATE	DESCRIPTION OF TRANSACTION	PAYMENT/DEBIT (-)	√ T	FEE (IF ANY) (-)	DEPOSIT/CREDIT (+)	9000	00
	4/1	70.00, 60.00, 70.00, 80.00 10, 12, 15, 8				280 00	280 9280	00 00
110	4/1	John Anders	20 00				20 9260	00 00
111	4/1	City Water	160 00				160 9100	00 00
112	4/3	Mae Sennet	100 00				100 9000	00 00
113	4/4	Klein Nursery	200 00				8800	00
	4/11	70.00, 100.00, 90.00, 80.00 6, 7, 4, 1				340 00	9140	00

CONDOMINIUM OWNERS ASSN.   1344

P. O. BOX
FLO   9   11/1   19 90   96- / 1232

PAY TO THE
ORDER OF   Power Company $ 20.07

Twenty & 7/100   DOLLARS

HEAD OFFICE   VALLEY BANK
BOX · 9
FLO   9

MEMO   Signature

⑆ 20 ⑆931⑆ 49 2   9 6⑆ 1 4

80

Unit Owner Ledger

This book, too, is standard and simple, its only purpose being to show the money (mostly dues) paid by or to the unit owner. It includes the date, unit number and purpose of the transaction. Like the checkbook, it must be entered whenever a transaction is made, but usually retroactively at the end of the month.

NAME	Edward Dern				ACCT. NO. Unit 4			
ADDRESS	Box no., City, State, Zip				SHEET NO.			
		TERMS		CREDIT LIMIT			RATING	
DATE	ITEMS	FOL.	✓	DEBITS		CREDITS	DR CR	BALANCE
7/1 89	July payment rec'd					80 00		-0-
8/1	Aug dues			80 00				80 00
8/6	Payment rec'd					80 00		-0-
9/1	Sept dues			80 00				80 00
9/8	Payment rec'd					80 00		-0-
10/1	Oct dues			80 00				80 00
10/6	Payment rec'd					80 00		-0-
11/1	Nov dues			80 00				80 00
11/3	Payment rec'd					80 00		-0-
12/1	Dec dues			80 00				80 00
12/3	Payment rec'd					80 00		-0-
1/1 90	Jan dues			83 00				83 00
1/1	Payment rec'd					83 00		-0-
2/1	Feb dues			83 00				83 00
2/1	Payment rec'd					83 00		-0-
3/1	Mar dues			83 00				83 00
3/8	Payment rec'd					83 00		-0-
4/1	Apr dues			83 00				83 00
4/4	Payment rec'd					83 00		-0-
5/1	May dues			83 00				83 00
5/1	Payment rec'd					83 00		-0-

Analysis Ledger

This ledger is the heart of the bookkeeping for our condominium. It begins with columns for the six basic accounts (in which expense items are shown in red ink); plus one column for miscellaneous accounts (in the margin)--then one for the check or unit owner number; one for the item of expense or income; one for the date; one for the debits (charges, usually dues); one for the credits; and finally, one for the balance.

When entrees have been made in the above columns, the total of the dues column is distributed to individual accounts according to the percentages shown on the dues apportionment sheet; these totals are underlined in pencil. Of course, totals are written for all columns. To check the work, the sum of account totals (balances), including miscellaneous, must equal the difference between total charges and total credits, or bank balance. Monthly and accumulated totals are shown, and the bank balance must agree with the accumulated total.

To save work and clutter, the individual dues payments are not distributed to the accounts, only the total.

The joy of this analysis ledger is that it shows at a glance the amount of money left in the bank, lost in expenditures, gained in incomes and remaining in each account.

Bank

Item	Misc.	Est. Maint & Repair	Garbage & Grounds	Common Utilities	Insurance	Admin & Legal	Deferred Maint.	Unit Name	Date 1989	DESCRIPTION	CHARGES	CREDITS	BALANCE
1		185.69	52.44	656.29	472.79			1	A	7/1	7321.59	2932.68	13473.19
2								2	B	1	31.91		
3								3	C	1	58.75		
4								4	D	1	104.62		
5								5	E	7/4	104.62		
6								6	F	4	217.65		
7								7	G	4	72.55		
8								8	H	4	72.55		
9								9	I	4	73.53		
10								10	J	4	67.88		
11		(82.80)							Elec.	7/1	77.34	82.80	
12			(45.00)					11	City Disp	7	66.90	180.46	
13				(180.46)				12	K	7/11	77.34	45.00	
14								13	L	11	101.13		
15								14	M	11	101.13		
16								15	N	11	87.99		
17				(17.70)					O	11		17.70	
18								16	P	8	203.64		
19									Power	7/12	52.43		
20									Int.	7/12	159.96		
22	Legal 44.17 Exch. 100.00	280.02	12.035	303.58	547.79	138.36	20.86				1265.80	326.16	
23		2053.71	599.79	761.51	5253.58	3077.0	372.13				9423.55	3155.84	14738.99
24			(26.70)			(18.00)			Nursery	7/1		26.70	
25						(87.43)			Pest.	7/24		18.05	
26			(11.23)						Error Sv.	24		106.64	
27			(66.00)	19.24	36.00	9.09	138.27.4		Bin	7/25	104.62	66.00	
28		18.41	791							7/27			
		2072.32	50.377	781.45	5289.58	120.33	379.40				9528.17	337.623	14626.22

Budget

The first following table is called the budget, but it presents the development procedure as well. The budget is one of the most important parts of condominium bookkeeping because it imvolves the spending of unit owner money, and that is extremely important to the owners. Therefore, the maximum number of people should be involved in order to get it right and to develop the feeling that it is their own budget.

Although the board of directors should do this work, it can easily end up being done by only one director and a secretary-treasurer-bookkeeper, as at our River View Condominium. Still, frequent contact is made with the other directors. A larger condominium would have in the board a finance committee that might even have a budget committee to do basic work.

This work, of course, is to review all accounts to see where the money is going, to devise procedures and to carry out the wishes of the owners as expeditiously as posible. The owners should be kept informed, involved and satisfied by letters, memos and questionaires.

Here, the budget for 1991 has been prepared from the analysis ledger and the budget for 1990. First appears the column of account names, then one for the 1990 budget, one for 12-month expenses through June 1990 and one for the amounts in accounts at the end of June 1990; next come two columns of estimated expenses and income from June through December 1990 and, last, a column for the proposed budget for 1991.

The budget column is estimated from the

other columns. Estimated income, less estimated expenses, is added to amount in account to show money available at year's end. This money is then compared with the best guess for expenses in 1991, and the difference is the basis for the 1991 budget.

Statement of Expenses and Income

The statement of expenses and income is prepared at the end of the year, and is mostly self-explanatory, as shown on the second following table.

The various amounts of income for the year are totaled near the bottom of the chart. Also, the bank checking account balance is shown for both the beginning and the end of the year; difference here should equal the difference between income and expense for this intervening period.

CONDOMINIUM
PROPOSED BUDGET FOR 1991
saved as 5BUD91.CRP

	Budget for 90 Yearly	Expenses to 6-21-90 (12 mos.)	Amt. in accn't 6/21/90	6/21 to 12/31/90 Estimated expenses.	Est. Income	Proposed Budget 1991
ADMINISTRATIVE EXPENSES						
1. INSURANCE						
a. Mutual of E	$ ____.__	$ __4601.00		$ __4700.00		$ __4700.00
b. National Flood	_____.__	___829.00		___693.00		___793.00
Total	$ __6960.24	$ ___5430.00	__6344.23	__5393.00	__4060.00	$ __5493.00
2. Office						
a. I.R.S.	_____.__	___173.17		_____.__		___225.00
b. Mailing	_____.__	___103.00		_____.__		___75.00
c. Legal	_____.__	___50.00		_____.__		___300.00
d. Manager	_____.__	__1117.20		_____.__		__1270.00
Total	__1856.04	__1414.22	__1443.37	__1390.01	__1090.84	__1083.00	__1870.00
OPERATING EXPENSES						
1. Repair & Maintenance				paint 1&2 200.00		
a. Sprinkler system		__2316.00		paint 1 489.32		
b. Other		__1119.39		leaks 200.00		
				power wash 350.00		
				paint 1 800.00		
				window wash 130.00		
				chimneys 150.00		
				vents 100.00		
				caulking 100.00		
				roof 100.00		
Total	__3076.32	__3435.39	__1516.02	__2619.32	__1794.00	__3889.32
2. Garbage & Grounds						
a. Garbage		___640.50		___400.00		
b. Grounds		___953.27		gardener 1350.00		
				supplies 400.00		
				stones & ties 350.00		
Total	__2051.28	__1593.77	___595.85	__2500.00	__1197.00	__3150.00
3. Utilities						
a. Water & Sewer	_____.__	__2361.95				_____.__
b. P. (lights)	_____.__	___338.37				_____.__
Total	__3358.44	__2700.32	__1255.33	__1840.00	__1959.00	__2900.00
4. Deferred Maintenance	__2433.58	-0-	__5813.77			__2433.48
5. Operating Reserve (full)		-0-	__1000.00			_____.__
6. Misc., Dues refund			___104.59			
TOTAL (grand)	$__19735.80	$	$__14707.44	$__17915.21		$__19735.80

BALANCES
INCOME   S.V.B. acct.$____19146.46   M.L. int. $394.00   Total $19540.46
EXPENDITURES $____14707.44   14707.44
                       ─────────────   ─────────
                                                                    $ 4833.02

CHECKING
    S.   6/23/89 $___13476.19   (M   h   acct.$_____-0--.00) =$13476.19
    S.   6/21/90 $___10915.21   M   .h w acct $_____7394.00 = 18309.21
                                         Gain   _____
                                                                     4833.02
Note: Deferred Maint. 6/90 $___ 5813.77   2294.30
                       6/89 $___ 3519.47   ─────────
          Gain $___ 2294.30   Gain minus Def. Maint. $_2538.72

CONDOMINIUM (SE^I89.PRP)
STATEMENT OF EXPENSES & INCOME, 1989

Unit Owner's Expenses
Disbursed   Total

S. .12/29/88 $8474.28

ADMINISTRATIVE EXPENSES
  1. Insurance $5402.00
  2. Office   130.41
  3. Administrative   1039.56
  4. I.R.S.   92.00
  5. Legal   50.00
Total $6713.97

OPERATING EXPENSES
  1. Repair & Maintenance
     A. Sprinklers,   Nursery   2316.00
     B. Misc. (Electric, window cleaning,etc.) 190.60
                          Total   2506.60
  2. Garbage & Grounds
     A. Garbage-   Sanitary   532.50
     B. Grounds   952.89
        a. Supplies $386.39
        b. Gardener(John B   )   489.00
        d. Sign(CarolP   )   77.50
                          Total   1485.39
  3. Utilities
     A. Water & Sewer   2377.16
     B Outside Lights   260.10
                          Total   2637.26
  4. Deferred Maintenance ($4460.27)   -0.-   -0.-
  5. Operating Reserve (full $1000.00)   -0.-

                    Grand Total $13,343.22

****
                         INCOME

INCOME
  1. U.O. Dues   I,II&III $15,885.59 (out $87.99)(plus $26.50)
  3. Insurance   refund   36.00
  5.   Bank Interest   441.06

Total $16,362.65
****
  .Bank 12/31/89 $4493.71
Merrill Lynch.   12/29/89 $7,216.01. (Dividends $216.01).

        11,493.71
         8474.28
         3019.43

              16,362.65
              13,343.22
               3 019.43

Dues Apportionment Statement

The dues apportionment and other remaining items of bookkeeping are based on information already presented.

The following chart, made from the budget, presents the monthly expenses and their distribution as dues to each unit owner for the year 1991. These monthly amounts were taken from the budget as follows: Insurance at 5493.00 was divided by 12 and reduced to the 457.75; office expense at 1870.00 was reduced to 155.83; repair and maintenance at 3889.32 was reduced to 324.11, and so on.

Across the top of the chart is shown the anticipated cost for each account, such as exterior maintenance and repair or common utilities. These are totaled, converted to percentages, and shown underneath in the next line.

The first column of the chart lists the unit owners by unit number; the next column shows the unit area in square feet; and the third, converts the area to percent of the total condominium area. In the remaining columns, these percentages are applied to the account totals to arrive at the individual unit owner share in the cost of each account.

UNIT OWNER'S BUDGET

1991

(With Area of 24335 Sq.Ft.
the Dues-breakdown.)
(saved as UOL 9182.CAL)

C	D	E	H	I	J	K	L	M	N
DUES & UNIT OWNERS	AREA (Sq. Ft.)	"AREA" SHARE (%)	EXTERIOR MAINT. & REPAIR	GARBAGE & GROUNDS	COMMON UTILITIES	INSUR- ANCE	ADM. SEC. LEGAL OFFICE	DEFERRED MAINT.	TOTAL (Col. H Thru. M)
Breakdown of Monthly-Due Sum Amount......			$324.11	$262.50	$241.67	$457.75	$155.83	$202.79	$1644.65
(As Percent of Full Monthly Collection)..			19.71	15.96	14.69	27.83	9.48	12.33	100.00
1 H	761	3.12718	$10.14	$8.21	$7.56	$14.31	$4.87	$6.34	$51.43
2 P	1539	6.32422	$20.50	$16.60	$15.28	$28.95	$9.86	$12.82	$104.01
3 B	1104	4.53668	$14.70	$11.91	$10.96	$20.77	$7.07	$9.20	$74.61
4 S	1592	6.54202	$21.20	$17.17	$15.81	$29.95	$10.19	$13.27	$107.59
5 R	1104	4.53668	$14.70	$11.91	$10.96	$20.77	$7.07	$9.20	$74.61
6 M	1592	6.54202	$21.20	$17.17	$15.81	$29.95	$10.19	$13.27	$107.59
7 S	1104	4.53668	$14.70	$11.91	$10.96	$20.77	$7.07	$9.20	$74.61
8 B	1539	6.32422	$20.50	$16.60	$15.28	$28.95	$9.86	$12.82	$104.01
9 S	1119	4.59832	$14.90	$12.07	$11.11	$21.05	$7.17	$9.32	$75.62
10 B	790	3.24635	$10.52	$8.52	$7.85	$14.86	$5.06	$6.58	$53.39
11 S	894	3.67372	$11.91	$9.64	$8.88	$16.82	$5.72	$7.45	$60.42
12 M	1018	4.18328	$13.56	$10.98	$10.11	$19.15	$6.52	$8.48	$68.80
13 D	1339	5.50236	$17.83	$14.44	$13.30	$25.19	$8.57	$11.16	$90.49
14 M	1033	4.24491	$13.76	$11.14	$10.26	$19.43	$6.61	$8.61	$69.81
15 W	1033	4.24491	$13.76	$11.14	$10.26	$19.43	$6.61	$8.61	$69.81
16 F	1177	4.83666	$15.68	$12.70	$11.69	$22.14	$7.54	$9.81	$79.55
17 S	1177	4.83666	$15.68	$12.70	$11.69	$22.14	$7.54	$9.81	$79.55
18	1033	4.24491	$13.76	$11.14	$10.26	$19.43	$6.61	$8.61	$69.81
19 B	1033	4.24491	$13.76	$11.14	$10.26	$19.43	$6.61	$8.61	$69.81
20	1177	4.83666	$15.68	$12.70	$11.69	$22.14	$7.54	$9.81	$79.55
21 C	1177	4.83666	$15.68	$12.70	$11.69	$22.14	$7.54	$9.81	$79.55
	24335	100.00	$324.11	$262.50	$241.67	$457.75	$155.83	$202.79	$1644.65

Balance Sheet

This sheet presents the net worth of the condominium, or total assets, which is equal to the sum of liabilities and members equity. The assets consist of cash in the bank, plus restricted cash, such as that reserved for capital replacement of common elements; any dues still unpaid; the value of all buildings, which is their cost less accumulated depreciation; the estimated value of equipment; and capital improvements, such as the sea wall and new roofs, less their depreciation.

The only liabilities are accounts payable.

Members equity consists of the unrestricted cash; plus the investment in common area, buildings, and equipment; plus the reserve for capital replacement of common elements.

Unit Owners Association
BALANCE SHEET
June 30, 1990

ASSETS		FUNDS
Cash	$ 12,495	
Restricted Cash Total	5,814	$ 18,309
Dues Receivable		0
Common Area Buildings, Net of Accumulated Depreciation of $ 194,213		1,459,687
Equipment		200
Capital Improvements		
Sea Wall, Net of $ 734 Depreciation		6,396
Roofs, I and II, Net of $ 1335 Depreciation		18,251
TOTAL ASSETS		$ 1,502,843

LIABILITIES

Accounts Payable	$ 0

MEMBERS EQUITY

Unrestricted	12,495
Restricted	
Investment in Common Area, Buildings and Equipment	1,484.534
Reserve for Capital Replacement of Common Elements	5,814
TOTAL LIABILITIES AND MEMBERS' EQUITY	$ 1,502,843

Income Tax

This final item of bookkeeping is a simple preparation, made on Form 1120-H, and due on March 15 each year. An Association director has been doing it for our condominium.

The tax is levied on interest received from bank and other accounts holding money of the condominium.

Form 1120-H

Department of the Treasury
Internal Revenue Service

U.S. Income Tax Return for Homeowners Associations

► For Paperwork Reduction Act Notice, see instructions on page 2.

OMB No. 1545-0127

1987

For calendar year 1987 or tax year beginning _____, 1987, and ending _____, 19

Use IRS label. Otherwise, please print or type.
YK 93-0 103 8712 S29 9999 Y
UNIT OWNERS ASSOCIATION OF
CONDOMINIUM
PO BOX
FL   9

Employer Identification number (see instructions)

Date association formed 10/29/81

Check applicable boxes: (1) ☐ Final return (2) ☐ Change in address (3) ☐ Amended return

A	Total exempt function income. Must meet 60% gross income test (see instructions)	A	17,386
B	Total expenditures made for purposes described in 90% expenditure test (see instructions)	B	15,606
C	Association's total expenditures for the tax year (see instructions)	C	15,606
D	Enter the amount of tax-exempt interest received or accrued during the tax year	D	

Gross Income (excluding exempt function income)

1	Dividends	1	
2	Taxable interest	2	412
3	Gross rents	3	
4	Gross royalties	4	
5	Capital gain net income (attach Schedule D (Form 1120))	5	
6	Net gain (or loss) from Part II, Form 4797 (attach Form 4797)	6	
7	Other income (excluding exempt function income) (attach schedule)	7	
8	Gross income (excluding exempt function income) (add lines 1 through 7)	8	412

Deductions (directly connected to the production of gross income, excluding exempt function income)

9	Salaries and wages	9	
10	Repairs	10	
11	Rents	11	
12	Taxes	12	See Notes 1986
13	Interest	13	
14	Depreciation (attach Form 4562)	14	
15	Other deductions (attach schedule)	15	
16	Total deductions (add lines 9 through 15)	16	0
17	Taxable income before specific deduction of $100 (subtract line 16 from line 8)	17	412
18	Specific deduction of $100	18	$100
19	Taxable income (subtract line 18 from line 17)	19	312

Tax Computation

20	Enter 30% of line 19	20	94
21	Credits (see instructions)	21	
22	Total Tax—Subtract line 21 from line 20	22	94
23	Payments: a 1986 overpayment credited to 1987	23a	
	b 1987 estimated tax payments	23b	
	c Total ►	23c	
	d Tax deposited with Form 7004	23d	
	e Credit from regulated investment companies (attach Form 2439)	23e	
	f Credit for Federal tax on gasoline and special fuels (attach Form 4136)	23f	
	g Add lines 23c through 23f	23g	
24	Tax due (subtract line 23g from line 22). See instruction D4 for depositary method of payment	24	94
25	Overpayment (subtract line 22 from line 23g)	25	
26	Enter amount of line 25 you want: Credited to 1988 estimated tax ► Refunded ►	26	

Please Sign Here

Under penalties of perjury, I declare that I have examined this return, including accompanying schedules and statements, and to the best of my knowledge and belief, it is true, correct, and complete. Declaration of preparer (other than taxpayer) is based on all information of which preparer has any knowledge.

Signature of officer _____ Date 2/23/88 Title Manager

Paid Preparer's Use Only

Preparer's signature: John Date 2/23/88 Check if self-employed ☐
Preparer's social security no. 5 : 18 : 0
Firm's name (or yours if self-employed) and address
E.I. No. ►
ZIP code ►

Form **1120-H** (1987)

8

LIVING

LIVING

There is something neat about a condominium--delightful the way each person has his or her own unit, private and free, yet all the while having a part in the larger organization. This kind of living satisfies everyone's desire to own a home and belong to a club, to share in all the action.

Of course, problems will occur, brought on by such things as weather damage, disagreements, selfishness both among unit owners and developers, law suits, unwillingness to share the work, poor management, lack of cooperation, excessive individuality, renters arguments, absentee owners and lack of communication. But much of this is part of living anywhere.

On the other hand, where else can you afford clubhouse facilities like swimming pools, a hot spa and sauna, billiards, bingo, coffee; all indoors. And outdoors: tennis courts, handball, and trailer parking. Also, don't forget the club activities like breakfasts and luncheons, picnics and parties, dances and shows. There are even clubs within clubs like the travel club, mens club and womens club. All of this is affordable simply because so many share the costs--the larger the condominiunm the lower the cost per person. Even the smallest condominium, without a club room, can still afford club activities.

Condominium living brings many people together in close proximity to desirable places such as schools, shopping centers and even the work place. This comes at a time when suitable space for other styles of living is hard to find, and the cost is prohibitive. Condominiums also benefit the larger communities around them, often bringing life once more to dying city centers.

It should be noted that living similar to that of condominiums can sometimes be found in large apartment complexes where the managers provide amenities and spare renters many of the problems. However, this is more expensive and does not respond quite as well to the desires of the renters.

Renting (as opposed to owning) a condominium is not a bad idea from the viewpoint of the renter, but in a number of ways it is not so good for the association. Renters move more, and have less interest in the affairs and upkeep of the property. Also, for every renter there is one less owner close enough to serve on the board.

Living is necessarily affected by government, and it is interesting to note that the condominium adds one more level to our many levels of government. First comes the family, then the condominium, then, in turn, the city, county, state, nation and united nations.

Condominiums have now had some thirty years to improve--Laws, rules and regulations have been made and remade; builders and developers have learned much; and the actual living experience has been documented. More of the same needs to be done.

Condominiums have provided one more career possibility: that of professional manager. Few of these people are available, the need for them is great, the work may be hard, but the rewards can be considerable.

Condominium living is here to stay. It is satisfying and people like it.

APPENDIX A -- ORS

APPENDIX A -- ORS

Declarant Requirements	103
Powers of the Association	103
Contents of Bylaws	106
Insurance	108
Lien Against Unit	108
Association Records	109
Boundaries of Unit	109
Interest in Common Elements	110
Allocation of Common Expenses	111
Maintenance and Improvement of Units	111
Use and Maintenance of Common Elements	112
Service of Process	113
Taxation of Units	113
Disclosure by Developer	114
Added Information by Developer	115
Public Report	116
Requirements for Sale	117
Cancellation of Sale of Unit	118
Notice of Cancellation Rights	118

APPENDIX A

OREGON REVISED STATUTES (ORS)

These begin by specifying warranties against defects in the new construction, and then present the creation of unit ownership. Property is submitted to unit ownership by declaration, the contents of which are enumerated. The declaration must next be approved and recorded. Then required are supplemental information for additional development and for amendments to the declaration, and finally, approval by the commissioner and owners.

The requirements continue as follows, including explanations and descriptions:

The declarant will hold an easement through common elements as needed for any special right.

The declarant shall establish a reserve account for replacement of those common elements that will normally require replacement in from three to 30 years.

The declarant may provide for a period of declarant control of the association of unit owners.

For turnover of declarant control to association control, a transitional committee shall be established if the number of units will total at least 20.

A turnover meeting shall be called by the declarant within 90 days of the expiration of any period of declarant control reserved in the declaration.

A successor declarant is subject to all obligations and liabilities imposed on a declarant.

Powers of the association of unit owners:

(1) An association of unit owners shall be organized to serve as a means through which the unit owners may take action with regard to the administration, management and operation

of the condominium. The association shall be organized as a corporation for profit, or as a non-profit corporation, or as an unincorporated association.

(2) Membership in the association of unit owners shall be limited to unit owners.

(3) The affairs of the association shall be governed by a board of directors as provided for in the bylaws.

(4) Subject to the provisions of the condominium's declaration and bylaws, and whether or not the association is unincorporated, the association may:

(a) Adopt and amend bylaws and rules and regulations;

(b) Adopt and amend budgets for revenues, expenditures and reserves and levy and collect assessments for common expenses from unit owners;

(c) Hire and terminate managing agents and other employees, agents and independent contractors;

(d) Institute, defend or intervene in litigation or administrative proceedings in its own name on behalf of itself or on behalf of two or more unit owners on matters affecting the condominium;

(e) Make contracts and incur liabilities;

(f) Regulate the use, maintenance, repair, replacement and modification of common elements;

(g) Cause additional improvement to be made as a part of the common elements;

(h) Acquire by purchase, lease, devise, gift or voluntary grant real property or any interest therein and take, hold, possess and dispose of real property or any interest therein;

(i) Impose and receive any payments, fees or charges for the use, rental or operation of the common elements;

(j) Impose charges for late payments

of assessments, attorney fees for collection of assessments and, after giving notice and an opportunity to be heard, levy reasonable fines for violations of the declaration, bylaws and rules and regulations of the association;

(k) Impose reasonable charges for the preparation and recordation of amendments to the declaration or statements of unpaid assessments;

(l) Provide for the indemnification of its officers and executive board and maintain directors' and officers' liability insurance;

(m) Exercise any other powers conferred by the declaration or bylaws;

(n) Exercise all other powers that may be exercised in this state by any such association; and

(o) Exercise any other powers determined by the association to be necessary and proper for the governance and operation of the association.

(5) Subject to subsection (6) of this section, unless expressly prohibited by the declaration, the association has the authority to execute, acknowledge, deliver and record on behalf of the unit owners easements, rights of way, licenses and other similar interests affecting the general common elements.

(6) The granting of any interest pursuant to subsection (5) of this section shall be first approved by at least 75 percent ofthe unit owners.

(7) The instrument granting an interest pursuant to subsection (5) of this section shall be executed by the chairman and secretary of the association and acknowledged in the manner provided for acknowledgment of such instruments by such officers and shall state that such grant was approved by at least 75 percent of the unit owners.

The declarant shall adopt and record on

behalf of the association the initial bylaws which shall govern the administration of the condominium; an amendment of the bylaws shall not be effective unless approved by at least a majority of the unit owners and recorded; in condominiums which are exclusively residential, the bylaws may not provide that greater than a majority is required to amend the bylaws except for amendments relating to age restrictions, pet restrictions, limitations on the number of persons who may occupy units and limitations on the rental or leasing of units; the bylaws may not be amended to limit or diminish any special declarant right without the consent of the declarant; and before any amended bylaws or amendment to a bylaw may be recorded, it must be approved by the Real Estate Commissioner.

Contents of bylaws; they shall provide for:

(1) The organization of the association of unit owners in the initial meeting and the method of calling that meeting.

(2) The formation of a transitional committee.

(3) The turnover meeting, including when the meeting shall be called, the method of calling the meeting, the right of a unit owner to call the meeting and a statement of the purpose of the meeting.

(4) The method of calling all other meetings of the unit owners and the percentage that shall constitute a quorum.

(5) The election from among the unit owners of a board of directors and the number of persons constituting the board; the powers and duties of the board; the compensation, if any, of the directors; and the method of removal from office of directors.

(6) The method of calling meetings of the board of directors and a statement that

all meetings of the board of directors of the association of unit owners shall be open to unit owners.

(7) The election of a chairman, a secretary and a treasurer.

(8) The maintenance, upkeep and repair of the common elements and payment for the expense thereof, including the method of approving payment vouchers.

(9) The employment of personnel necessary for the maintenance, upkeep and repair of the common elements.

(10) The manner of collecting from the unit owners their share of the common expenses.

(11) Insurance coverage in accordance with ORS.

(12) The preparation and distribution of the annual financial statement in accordance with ORS.

(13) The filing of an Annual Report and any amendment with the Secretary of State.

(14) The method of adopting and amending administrative rules and regulations governing the details of operation and use of the common elements.

(15) Such restrictions on enjoyment and maintenance of units and common elements as will not unreasonably interfere with their proper use.

(16) Any restrictions on use or occupancy of units.

(17) The method of amending the bylaws subject to ORS.

(18) Any other details regarding the property that the declarant considers desirable. However, if a provision required to be in the declaration is included in the bylaws, the voting requirements for amending the declaration shall also govern the amendment of the provision in the bylaws.

(19) The method of apportioning common expenses in the event new units are to be ad-

ded during the course of the year.

All meetings of the board of directors of the association of unit owners shall be open to unit owners. Meetings may be conducted by telephone.

The deed of a unit shall contain the name of the property, the recording index numbers and the date of recording of the declaration or supplemental declaration; the unit designation; and any further details the grantor and grantee may consider desirable.

The board of dirctors shall obtain and maintain at all times and shall pay for out of the common expense funds, the following **insurance** covering both the common elements and individual units:

(a) Property insurance including, but not limited to, fire, extended coverage, vandalism and malicious mischief; and

(b) Insurance covering the legal liability of the association of unit owners, the unit owners individually and the manager including, but not limited to, the board of directors, the public and the unit owners and their invitees or tenants, incident to ownership, supervision, control or use of the property.

Lien of association against unit:

(1) The association shall have a lien against any unit for non-payment of common expenses and interest; it shall take effect upon recording in the county a claim containing all details of the debt; and the lien shall be prior to all others except tax liens and a first mortgage or trust deed of record.

(2) When a claim has been filed, subsequent unpaid assessments and interest shall accumulate without the need of further filing.

(3) A lien may continue in force for not more than six years from its filing date, which is deemed to be the date the assessment became due.

(4) In a foreclosure suit against a

unit the owner shall pay rent, if provided by the bylaws, and the association manager may bid in the unit at the foreclosure sale, unless forbidden by the declaration.

The association shall keep records as follows:

(1) It shall keep all papers received at the turnover meeting.

(2) It shall keep financial records sufficient for proper accounting purposes.

(3) Within 90 days after the end of the fiscal year, the board of directors shall distribute to each unit owner a copy of the annual financial statement consisting of a balance sheet and income and expense statement for the preceding fiscal year.

(4) All these records shall be reasonably available for examination by unit owners and mortgagees, and the association shall maintain a copy, suitable for duplication, of the following:

(a) the declaration, bylaws, and amendments;

(b) the most recent annual financial statement;

(c) the current operating budget;

Association agreements made before the turnover meeting shall cease within three years; if made after January 1, 1982, the board can terminate them upon 30 days' written notice given within 60 days after the turnover meeting.

Each unit owner shall be entitled to exclusive ownership, possession, sale, or encumbrance of his unit as if it were sole and entirely independent of the other units.

Unless otherwise provided in the declaration, if the declaration designates walls, floors or ceilings as <u>boundaries of a unit</u>:

(1) All lath, furring, wallboard, plasterboard, plaster, paneling, tiles, wallpaper, paint, finished flooring and any other materials constituting any part of the finished

surfaces thereof shall be a part of the unit, and all other portions of the walls, floors or ceilings shall be a part of the common elements.

(2) The following shall be a part of the unit:

(a) all spaces, nonbearing interior partitions windows, window frames, exterior doors, door frames and all other fixtures and improvements within the boundaries of the unit; and

(b) all outlets of utility service lines, including but not limited to power, light, gas, hot and cold water, heating, refrigeration, air conditioning, and waste disposal within the boundaries of the unit.

Rules concerning <u>interest of units in common elements</u>:

(1) Each unit shall be entitled to an undivided interest in the common elements in the allocation expressed in the declaration. Such allocation shall be expressed as a percentage of undivided interest in the common elements, and it shall not be altered unless all unit owners having an interest in the particular common element agree thereto and record an amendment to the declaration setting forth the altered allocation of each unit having an interest.

(2) The sums of the undivided interest in the common elements shall equal 100 percent.

(3) The undivided interest in the common elements shall be conveyed or encumbered with the unit.

(4) The common elements shall remain undivided.

(5) Except where expressly prohibited by the declaration or bylaws, the right of use of any unit in a limited common element may be transferred to any other unit. Such transfer shall occur only if the existing unit owner and mortgagee agree to and record an amendment

to the declaration, setting forth the transfer.

Unless otherwise provided in the declaration, each unit shall be entitled to one vote.

Allocation of common expenses:

(1) Unless otherwise provided in the declaration, the common expenses shall be charged to the unit owners according to the allocation of undivided interest of each unit in the common elements.

(2) No unit owner may escape common expense by claiming waiver of use or enjoyment of any of the common elements or by abandonment of the unit.

(3) From the date that the declaration is recorded, the declarant shall pay assessments due for operating expenses and reserves on all unsold units; this includes reserves accrued at the time of initial sale to unit owner, but the declarant may require that the unit owner pay.

(4) The association shall not assess units owned by the declarant for additional capital improvements without the written consent of a declarant owning more than two units.

Maintenance and improvement of units:

(1) After acquiring an adjoining unit or part, a unit owner may submit a written request to the board of directors for permission to remove or alter any intervening partition or to create apertures therein, even if the partition in whole or in part is a common element. The board shall approve the change unless it determines within 45 days that the proposed change is damaging; in which case it may require the unit owner, at his own expense, to submit an opinion of a registered architect or registered professional engineer that the proposed change will not impair the structural integrity or mechanical systems of the condominium or lessen the support of any

portion of the condominium. Removal of partitions or creation of apertures under this paragraph is not an alteration of boundaries.

(2) A unit owner shall make no repair or alteration or perform. any other work on his unit which would jeopardize the soundness or safety of the property, reduce the value thereof, impair any easement or hereditament or increase the common expenses of the association, unless the consent of all the other unit owners affected is first obtained.

(3) Unless otherwise provided in the declaration or bylaws, a unit owner may not change the appearance of the common elements or the exterior appearance of a unit without permission of the board of directors of the association.

(4) Additional limitations may be specified by the declaration or the bylaws.

Use and maintenance of common elements:

(1) Each unit owner may use the common elements in accordance with the purposes for which they are intended, but may not hinder or encroach upon the lawful rights of the other unit owners.

(2) The necessary work of maintenance, repair, and replacement of the common elements, and additions or improvements, shall be carried out only as provided in the bylaws.

(3) The association of unit owners shall have the right to have access to each unit as may be necessary for the maintenance, repair, or replacement of the common elements, or to make emergency repairs therein necessary for the public safety, or to prevent damage to the common elements or to another unit.

Each unit owner and the declarant shall comply with the bylaws and with the administrative rules and regulations adopted pursuant thereto, and with the covenants, conditions, and restrictions in the declaration or in the deed to the unit. Failure to comply therewith shall be grounds for an action maintainable by the association of unit owners or by an aggrieved unit owner.

Actions by and against unit owners; service of process:

(1) Actions may be brought on behalf of two or more of the unit owners, as their respective interests may appear, by the manager with respect to any cause of action relating to the common elements or more than one unit. Service of process on two or more unit owners, in any action relating to the common elements or more than one unit, may be made on the person designated in the declaration to receive service of process, or in duplicate on the recording officer of the county in which the declaration is filed. The recording officer shall promptly send a copy of the document served by certified or registered mail to the person designated in the declaration to receive service of process.

(2) If the association of unit owners wishes to designate a person other than the one named in the declaration to receive service of process in the cases provided in subsection (1) of this section, it shall record an amendment to the declaration. The amendment shall be certified by the chairman and the secretary of the association of unit owners, and shall state the name of the successor with his residence or place of business and that the person named in the amendment was designated by resolution duly adopted by the association of unit owners.

Taxation of units:

(1) Each unit with its allocation of undivided interest in the common elements shall be considered a parcel of real property and assessed only in the name of the unit owner, subject to separate assessment and taxation by any taxing unit in like manner as other parcels of real property.

(2) In determining the true cash value of a unit with its undivided interest in the

common elements, the county assessor may use the allocation of undivided interest in the common elements appertaining to a unit as expressed in the declaration.

(3) Exemptions from executions and real property taxes apply to the owner of each unit or to the individual units, as the case may be.

Disclosure requirements by developer:

(1) The Real Estate Commissioner shall adopt rules to insure that each developer of a condominium discloses fully and accurately to prospective purchasers of condominium units all material circumstances or features affecting such condominium of which he should be aware by requiring that prior to sale or lease of a condominium unit the developer shall notify the commissioner of his intention to sell by way of a "Notice of Intention," which shall contain the following information:

(a) the name and address of the condominium and the name, address, and telephone number of the developer;

(b) a general narrative description of the condominium stating the total number and description of the units and a precise statement of the nature of the interest being offered;

(c) a general disclosure of the status of construction and the actual or scheduled dates of completion of buildings, recreation facilities, and other common elements;

(d) the significant terms of any financing offered by the developer to purchasers of the condominium units;

(e) a brief description of any warranties for structural elements and mechanical and other systems;

(f) a projection of the budget of the association of unit owners for the operation and maintenance and any other common expenses of the condominium;

(g) a description of any provisions

made in the budget of the condominium for reserves for capital expenditures for repair or replacement of common elements and an explanation of the basis for such reserves;

(h) a statement of significant provisions for management of the condominium including voting rights, meetings, and documents by which purchasers may be bound, including the declaration, bylaws, ground leases, management agreement, easements, covenants, restrictions and conditions; and

(i) a statement of the right of any purchaser to void the contract other than as provided by statute, any conditions for the return of deposit and a statement about any present litigation concerning the condominium.

The commissioner may require developer to furnish such additional information with the notice of intention as the commissioner determines to be necessary and for protection of the public, including but not limited to:

(1) A statement of the terms and conditions on which it is intended to transfer or dispose of the land or interest therein, together with copies of any contract, conveyance, lease, assignment or other instrument intended to be used.

(2) Copies of all sales pamphlets and literature to be used in connection with the condominium. And

(3) Any other information that the developer may desire to present.

The information required by the ORS and the commissioner shall be kept current by the developer, and material changes shall be reported within 10 days after the change occurs. All of this information shall be provided by the developer for as long as the developer retains any unsold interest in the condominium to which the information pertains.

Public report:

Unless the making of a public report has

been waived, the commissioner shall make an examination of the condominium and issue a public report of his findings prior to negotiating for its sale or lease. The public report shall contain all information required by the rules presented above under notice of intention to sell (disclosure requirements).

The public report shall contain the following notice in at least 8-point type below the above information:
NOTICE TO PROSPECTIVE PURCHASERS

THE PROJECTION OF THE BUDGET OF THE ASSOCIATION OF UNIT OWNERS FOR THE OPERATION AND MAINTENANCE AND OTHER COMMON EXPENSES OF THE CONDOMINIUM IS ONLY AN ESTIMATE, PREPARED WITH DUE CARE.

Where the above information indicates that no provision is made in the budget of the condominium for reserves for capital expenditures for repair or replacement of common elements, the public report shall contain a statement to that effect in at least 8-point type.

If it is found to be in the public interest, the commissioner may include in the public report any information relating to the nature of condominium interests in general or the condominium for which the public report is being issued.

With respect to any condominium in this state, if, after examination of the above information, the commissioner concludes that a public report is not necessary to protect the public, he shall waive the provisions of ORS that he considers unnecessary for the protection of the public. He shall notify the developer about the waiver within 15 days of receipt of the notice of intention. However, he may, for good and sufficient cause, revoke any waiver at any time upon 20 days' notice and a hearing held for such purpose.

A copy of the public report shall be given to the prospective purchaser by the developer not later than the date the unit sales agreement is fully executed by all parties. The developer shall take a receipt for the report and keep it on file subject to inspection by the commissioner for a period of three years from the date the receipt is taken.

Requirements for sale:

No condominium unit shall be sold by a developer by means of a land sale contract unless a collection escrow is established (and the commissioner allowed to inspect it) with a person or firm authorized to receive escrows and all of the following are deposited in the escrow: a copy of the title report or abstract; a true copy of the original sales document; a commitment to give a partial release from the terms and provisions of any blanket encumbrance; and a document in good and sufficient form transferring the interest purchased.

Before the unit sales agreement is fully executed by all parties, the developer shall deliver to the purchaser a copy of the declaration and bylaws of the condominium and any supplements and amendments thereto affecting the unit, and take a receipt for them. He shall also deliver, after execution of the agreement, a copy of the fully executed agreement that contains the "Notice to Purchaser". Finally he shall deliver, prior to the conveyance of the unit by deed, lease, or contract, any ground leases, leases with the association for recreation or parking facilities, and escrow instructions applying to the transaction.

Cancellation of sale of unit:

A purchaser of a condominium unit may cancel for any reason the sale of a condominium unit within five business days after the date on which the latest of the following events occurs:

(1) the signing by the purchaser of the unit sales agreement;

(2) the signing of the receipt for the public report; or

(3) the signing of the receipt for delivery of the papers required in the preceding paragraph.

Cancellation occurs when the purchaser of an interest gives written notice to the developer; if it is by mail, it must be by certified mail.

Upon receipt of timely notice of cancellation, the developer shall immediately return to the purchaser all payments received from the purchaser, who shall immediately transfer rights in the interest to the developer, unencumbered. Any evidence of indebtedness shall be returned and cancelled.

No act of a purchaser shall be effective to waive the right of cancellation, that terminates at the time of closing of the unit purchase transaction. At this time, a developer may require that a purchaser execute and deliver to the developer a signed statement disclaiming any notice of cancellation that may have been made.

A purchaser may waive the right of cancellation, in writing, after the unit sales agreement is fully executed by all parties. But this agreement shall not obligate a purchaser to waive the right of cancellation.

Notice to purchaser of cancellation rights:

A unit sales agreement shall contain, either upon the first page or upon a separate sheet attached to such first page, the following notice in at least 8-point type:

NOTICE TO PURCHASER

(RIGHT OF CANCELLATION)

BY SIGNING A UNIT SALES AGREEMENT YOU ARE INCURRING A CONTRACTUAL OBLIGATION TO PURCHASE AN INTEREST IN A CONDOMINIUM. HOWEVER, YOU HAVE THE RIGHT TO CANCEL THIS AGREEMENT FOR ANY REASON FOR FIVE BUSINESS DAYS (EXCLUDING SATURDAYS AND HOLIDAYS) AFTER WHICHEVER OF THE FOLLOWING IS LAST TO OCCUR:

(1) SIGNING BY THE PURCHASER OF THE UNIT SALES AGREEMENT;

(2) SIGNING BY THE PURCHASER OF THE RECEIPT FOR THE PUBLIC REPORT, IF ANY; OR

(3) SIGNING BY THE PURCHASER OF THE RECEIPT FOR A COPY OF THE CONDOMINIUM DECLAREATION AND BYLAWS AND ANY AMENDMENTS OR SUPPLEMENTS THERETO AFFECTING THE UNIT.

TO CANCEL THIS AGREEMENT, YOU MUST GIVE WRITTEN NOTICE TO THE DEVELOPER OR THE AGENT OF THE DEVELOPER AT THE FOLLOWING ADDRESS:

_____
_____
_____
_____
_____

(SUGGESTED PROCEDURE)

BEFORE EXECUTING THIS AGREEMENT, OR BEFORE THE CANCELLATION PERIOD ENDS, YOU SHOULD DO THE FOLLOWING:

(1) CAREFULLY EXAMINE THE PUBLIC REPORT, IF ANY, ISSUED BY THE REAL ESTATE COMMISSIONER ON THE CONDOMINIUM AND ALL ACCOMPANYING INFORMATION DELIVERED BY THE DEVELOPER. OREGON LAW REQUIRES THE DEVELOPER TO DELIVER TO YOU A COPY OF THE DECLARATION AND BYLAWS OF THE CONDOMINIUM AND ANY SUPPPLEMENTS AND AMENDMENTS THERETO AFFECTING THE UNIT PRIOR TO THE TIME THE UNIT SALES AGREEMENT IS FULLY EXECUTED BY ALL PARTIES. A COPY OF THE DECLARATION AND BYLAWS, AND ANY SUPPLEMENTS AND AMENDMENTS THERETO, ARE AVAILABLE FROM THE ASSOCIATION FOR EXAMINATION AND DUPLICATION, AT A REASON

ABLE FEE, UPON YOUR WRITTEN REQUST.

    (2) INQUIRE OF YOUR LENDER WHETHER YOU CAN GET ADEQUATE FINANCING ON AN ACCEPTABLE BASIS.

    (3) INQUIRE OF THE DEVELOPER AND THE LENDER WHAT THE AMOUNT OF THE CLOSING COSTS WILL BE.

    OREGON LAW REQUIRES THAT YOU IMMEDIATELY BE GIVEN A COPY OF THIS NOTICE AND A COPY OF THE UNIT SALES AGREEMENT WHEN IT HAS BEEN FULLY EXECUTED BY ALL PARTIES.

    A copy of the above notice shall be given to each purchaser, at the time of or immediately following the purchaser's signing of the unit sales agreement, for the use of the purchaser.

    A purchaser of a vendor's interest in a land sale contract for which the escrow has been established shall deposit in the escrow any instruments necessary to assure that the contract vendee can obtain the legal title bargained for upon compliance with the terms and conditions of the contract.

    A developer who has sold interests in a condominium under a land sale contract shall not dispose of or subsequently encumber his vendor's interest therein unless the terms of the instrument of disposition or the encumbrance provide the means by which the purchaser or holder of the encumbrance will comply with the preceding paragraph.

    Records of the sale of any condominium unit shall be subject to inspection by the commissioner and shall be made available to him in Oregon at his request.

APPENDIX B -- DECLARATION

APPENDIX B

DECLARATION

THIS DECLARATION, pursuant to the provisions of the oregon Unit Ownership Law, is made and executed this ____ day of _____, 1978 by River View DEVELOPOMENT CO., an Oregon partnership, hereinafter called "Developer."

Developer proposes to create a condominium to be known as River View, which will be located in _____, _____ County, Oregon. The purpose of this declaration is to submit Phase 1 of River View to the condominium form of ownership and use in the manner provided by the Oregon Unit Ownership Law.

NOW, THEREFORE, Developer does hereby declare and provide as follows:

1. DEFINITIONS. When used herein the following terms shall have the following meanings:

1.1 "Bylaws" means the Bylaws of the Association of Unit Owners of River View pursuant to Section 12 below as the same may be amended from time to time.

1.2 "Developer" means River View Development Co., an Oregon partnership, and its successors and assigns.

1.3 "Plans" means the plat or site plan and floor plans of Phase 1 of River View recorded simultaneously with the recording of this declaration.

1.4 "Incorporation by Reference." Except as otherwise provided in this declaration, each of the terms defined in ORS shall have the meanings set forth therein.

2. PROPERTY SUBMITTED. The property submitted to the Oregon Unit Owsnership Law hereunder is held by Developer and conveyed by it in fee simple estate. The land submitted hereunder, being Phase 1 of River View, is located in _____, _____ County, Oregon,

and is more particularly described in Exhibit A attached hereto. Such property includes the land so described, all buildings, improvements and structures thereon, all easements, rights and appurtenances belonging thereto, and all personal property used in connection therewith.

3. NAME. The name by which the property submitted hereunder shall be known is "River View."

4. UNITS.

4.1 "General Description of Buildings." Phase 1 contains one building of nine dwelling units. The dwelling unit building is 2-1/2 stories without basement. The building is of concrete masonry, concrete and wood frame.

4.2 "General Description, Location and Designation of Units." Phase 1 is shown in the plans filed simultaneously herewith and made a part of this declaration as if fully set forth herein. The approximate area of each unit is shown on Exhibit B, attached hereto and made a part hereof.

4.3 "Boundaries of Units." Each unit shall be bounded by the interior surfaces of its perimeter and bearing walls, floors, ceilings, windows and window frames, doors and door frames and trim, and shall include both the interior surfaces so described and the air space so encompassed. In addition, each unit shall include the outlet of any utility service lines, including water, sewerage, electricity and ventilating ducts, within the unit, but shall not include any part of such lines or ducts themselves.

5. GENERAL COMMON ELEMENTS. Each unit will be entitled to a percentage ownership interest in the general common elements determined by the ratio by which the approximate area of the particular unit bears to the total approximate area of all units combined, as is more particularly described in paragraph 13.4 below. The general common elements consist of

the following:

5.1 The land, pathways, driveways, fences, grounds, carport structures and parking areas, except parking spaces within carports bearing the number of a unit as shown on the plans, which are designated as limited common elements by Section 6 below.

5.2 Pipes, ducts, flues, chutes, conduits, wires and other utility installations to their outlets.

5.3 Roofs, foundations, bearing walls, perimeter walls, beams, columns and girders to the interior surfaces thereof.

5.4 The exterior surfaces of porches and decks.

5.5 All other elements of the buildings and the property necessary or convenient to their existence, maintenance and safety, or normally in common use, except as may be expressly designated herein as part of a unit or a limited common element.

6. LIMITED COMMON ELEMENTS. The following shall constitute limited common elements, the use of which shall be restricted to the units to which they pertain:

6.1 All porches and decks, except for the outside exterior surfaces thereof, each of which shall pertain to the unit which it adjoins.

6.2 Parking spaces within carport structures, each of which shall pertain to the unit whose number it bears in the Plans.

6.3 Storage areas on entry porches, decks and carports, each of which shall pertain to the unit which the specific porch or deck adjoins, or to which the adjoining parking space pertains in the case of storage areas in carports.

7. USE OF PROPERTY. Each unit is to be used for residential or lodging purposes, except that one unit may be used for activities relating to the sale or rental of other units, in the Condominium. Additional limitations on

use are contained in the Bylaws of the Association of Unit Owners of River View herewith and the rules and regulations adopted pursuant to such bylaws. Each unit owner shall be bound by each of the terms, conditions, limitations and provisions contained in such documents.

8. COMMON PROFITS AND EXPENSES; VOTING.

8.1 The common profits derived from and the common expenses of the common elements shall be distributed and charged to the owner of each unit according to the percentage of undivided interest of such unit in the general common elements.

8.2 Each unit owner shall be entitled to a vote in the affairs of the association of unit owners equal to his percentage of undivided interest in the general common elements for each unit owned by him.

9. SERVICE OF PROCESS. The name of the person to receive service of process in cases provided in ORS is _____ , and his place of business within _____ County, Oregon, is _____.

10. ENCROACHMENTS. If any portion of the common elements now encroaches upon any unit, or if any unit now encroaches upon any other unit or upon any portion of the common elements, as a result of the construction of any building, or if any such encroachment shall occur hereafter as a result of settling or shifting of any building, a valid easement for the encroachment and for the maintenance of the same so long as the building stands, shall exist. In the event any building, unit, adjoining unit, or adjoining common element, shall be partially or totally destroyed as a result of fire or other casualty or as a result of condemnation or eminent domain proceedings, and then rebuilt, encroachments of parts of the common elements upon any unit or of any unit upon any other unit or upon any portion of the common elements, due to such rebuilding, shall be permitted, and valid

easements for such encroachments and the maintenance thereof shall exist so long as the building shall stand.

11. APPROVAL BY MORTGAGEES. In addition to any other approvals required by the Oregon Unit Ownership Law, this declaration, or the bylaws of the association of unit owners, the prior written approval of all holdlers of first mortgages or beneficiaries of first deeds of trust of units in the condominium must be obtained for the following:

11.1 The removal of the property from unit ownership, except when such removal is by operation of ORS in the case of substantial loss to the units and common elements;

11.2 The partition or subdivision of any unit or of the common enements;

11.3 A change in the percentage interests in the common elements of the unit owners, except when such change is by virtue of the annexation of additional phases as provided in Section 13 below; or

11.4 Any amendment to this Section.

12. ADOPTION OF BYLAWS, APPOINTMENT OF INTERIM BOARD, AND DESIGNATION OF MANAGER. Upon the execution and the filing of this declaration, the Developer shall adopt bylaws for the Association of Unit Owners of River View, which bylaws are to be filed simultaneously herewith. At the same time, Developer will appoint an interim board of directors of the association, which directors shall serve until their successors have been elected as provided in the bylaws. Such interim board of directors may appoint a manager or managing agent for the condominium on behalf of the association of unit owners, and such manager or managing agent shall have the complete authority to assume full control and responsibility for the management, operation and maintenance of the condominium from the date of its formation at the expense of the associa-

tion.

13. PLAN OF DEVELOPMENT. The condominium may be developed in up to 8 phases. By filing this declaration, Developer hereby submits Phase 1 to the condomiuium form of ownership. Developer reserves the right to add 7 additional phases to the condomiuium and to annex such additional phases by filing supplements to this declaration pursuant to ORS.

13.1 Maximum Number of Units: Phase 1 contains a total of 9 units. Proposed Phase 2 would contain not more than 8 units; proposed Phase 3 would contain not more than 8 units; proposed Phase 4 would not contain more than 8 units; proposed Phase 5 would not contain more than 9 units: proposed Phase 6 would not contain more than 9 units; proposed Phase 7 would not contain more than 8 units; and proposed Phase 8 would not contain more than 8 units, for a total of not more than 66 units in the condominium.

13.2 Election Not to Proceed: In order to limit the condominium to fewer than eight phases, Developer may file a declaration in the Records of Deeds of _____ County, Oregon, by January 1, 1983, so stating. In any case, no additional phase may be added more than seven years after the filing of this declaration.

13.3 Additional Common Elements: Developer does not propose to include in Phases 2, 3, 4, 5, 6, 7, or 8 any common elements which would substantially increase the proportionate amount of the common expenses payable by owners of units in Phase 1.

13.4 Percentage Interest in Common Elements: The percentage interest in the common elements of units in Phase 1 will change if additional phases are annexed to the condominium. A chart showing the percentage interest in the common elements of each unit upon the filing of this declaration and after the annexation of each proposed phase is attached hereto as Exhibit C.

      13.5 Order of Development of Proposed Phases: The Developer reserves the right to change the order of development of the proposed phases without the necessity of complying with the formal amendment requirements of ORS.

      IN WITNESS WHEREOF, Developer has caused this declaration to be executed this _____ day of _____ , 1978.

                      RIVER VIEW DEVELOPMENT CO.,
                        An Oregon partnership

APPENDIX C -- BYLAWS

CONTENTS

APPENDIX C - BYLAWS

ARTICLE I: PLAN OF UNIT OWNERSHIP 134
Name and Location--Principal Office--Purposes--Applicability of Bylaws--Composition of Association.

ARTICLE II: MEETINGS OF ASSOCIATION 135
Place of Meetings--First Organizational Meeting--Annual Meetings--Special Meetings--Notice of Meetings--Voting--Proxies--Fiduciaries--and Joint Owners--Quorum of Unit Owners--Majority Vote--Order of Business.

ARTICLE III: BOARD OF DIRECTORS 139
Number and Qualification--Interim Directors--Election and Term of Office--Administrative Responsibility--Vacancies--Removal of Directors--Powers and Duties--Managing Agent or Manager--Organization Meeting--Regular and Special Meetings--Waiver of Notice--Quorum of Board of Directors--Presumption of Assent Compensation--Liability and Indemnification of Directors, Manager or Managing Agent--Fidelity Bonds--Insurance.

ARTICLE IV: OFFICERS 147
Designation--Election of Officers--Removal of Officers--Chairman--Secretary--Treasurer--Execution of Instruments--Compensation of Officers.

ARTICLE V: BUDGET, ESPENSES AND 149
ASSESSMENTS
Budget--Determination of Common Expenses--Special Assessments--Default in Payment of Common Expenses--Foreclosure of Liens for Unpaid Common Expenses--Statement of Common Expenses.

ARTICLE VI: RECORDS AND AUDITS 151
General Records--Records of Receipts and Expenditures--Assessment Roll--Payment of Vouchers--Reports and Audits--Notice of Sale, Mortgage or Lease.

ARTICLE VII: MAINTENANCE AND USE OF .... CONDOMINIUM PROPERTY 153
Maintenance and Repair--Additions, Alterations or Improvements--Damage or Destruction by Casualty of Condominium Property--Condemnation--Marina--Restrictions and Requirements Respecting use of Condominium Property--Right of Entry--Easements for Developer--Abatement and Enjoining of Violations.

ARTICLE VIII: AMENDMENTS TO BYLAWS 160
How Proposed--Adoption--Execution and Recording.

ARTICLE IX: MISCELLANEOUS 161
Notices--Waiver--Invalidity; Number; Captions --Definitions

APPENDIX C

BYLAWS
OF THE ASSOCIATION OF UNIT OWNERS
OF
RIVER VIEW

ARTICLE I: PLAN OF UNIT OWNERSHIP
1. NAME AND LOCATION. These are the bylaws of the ASSOCIATION OF UNIT OWNERS OF RIVER VIEW (hereinafter the "Association"). The RIVER VIEW (hereinafter the "Condominium") is located in _____ , _____ County, Oregon, and has been submitted to the Oregon Unit Ownership Law by a declaration filed simultaneously herewith and by supplemental declarations, if any, annexing property to the condominium (hereinafter collectively called "the declaration"). The location of the condomin-

ium is more specifically described in the declaration.

2. PRINCIPAL OFFICE. The principal office of the Association shall be located at the site of the condominium, _____ , Oregon.

3. PURPOSES. This Association is formed under the provisions of the Oregon Unit Ownership Law to serve as the means through which the unit owners may take action with regard to the administration, management and operation of the condominium.

4. APPLICABILITY OF BYLAWS. The Association, all unit owners and all persons using the condominium property shall be subject to these bylaws and to all rules and regulations which may be promulgated hereunder.

5. COMPOSITION OF ASSOCIATION. The Association shall be composed of all the unit owners of the condominium, including River View Development Co., a partnership, and its successors and assigns (hereinafter, "the developer"), and the Association itself, to the extent any of these own any units of the condominium.

ARTICLE II: MEETINGS OF ASSOCIATION

1. PLACE OF MEETINGS. The Association shall hold meetings at the office of the Asssociation, or such other suitable place convenient to the unit owners as may be designated by the board of directors from time to time.

2. FIRST ORGANIZATIONAL MEETING. Within one hundred and twenty (120) days after the developer has submitted the first phase of the condominium to unit ownership and adopted the initial bylaws the developer shall call the first meeting of the unit owners to organize the Association in the manner provided in Article II, Section 5, of these bylaws. In the event of lack of a quorum at such first organizational meeting, it may be adjourned to the time of the next annual meeting.

3. ANNUAL MEETINGS. The annual meetings of

the Association shall be held in the months of July or August at such hour and on such date as the chairman may designate, or if the chairman should fail to designate such date by the first day of July, then on the third Saturday in August. The annual meetings shall be for the purpose of electing directors and for the transaction of such other business as may properly come before the meeting.

4. SPECIAL MEETINGS. Special meetings of the Association may be called by the chairman or secretary or by a majority of the board of directors, and must be called by such officers upon receipt of a written request from at least thirty percent (30%) of the unit owners stating the purpose of the meeting. Business transacted at a special meeting shall be confined to the purposes stated in the notice.

5. NOTICE OF MEETINGS. Notice of all meetings of the Association stating the time and place and the objects for which the meeting is being called shall be given by the chairman or secretary. Such notice shall be in writing and mailed to each unit owner at his address as it appears on the books of the Association not less than ten (10) days nor more than sixty (60) days prior to the date of the meeting. Proof of such mailing shall be given by the affidavit of the person giving the notice. Notice of meeting may be waived by any unit owner before or after meetings. When a meeting is adjourned for less than 30 days, no notice of the adjourned meeting need be given other than by announcement at the meeting at which such adjournment takes place.

6. VOTING. Each unit owner shall have a vote equal to his percentage interest in the common elements of the condominium owned by him. The developer shall be entitled to vote as the unit owner of any then existing units retained by the developer, and the board of directors shall be entitled to vote on behalf of any unit which has been acquired by or on behalf

of the Association; provided, however, that the board of directors shall not be entitled to vote such units in any election of directors.

7. PROXIES. A vote may be cast in person or by proxy. A proxy given by a unit owner to any person who represents such owner at meetings of the Association shall be in writing and signed by such owner, and shall be filed with the secretary before or at the time of the meeting. No proxy shall be valid after the meeting for which it was solicited, unless otherwise expressly stated in the proxy, and every proxy shall automatically cease upon sale of the unit by its owner. A unit owner may pledge or assign his voting rights to a mortgagee. In such a case, the mortgagee or its designated representative shall be entitled to receive all notices to which the unit owner is entitled thereunder and to exercise the unit owner's voting rights from and after the time that the mortgagee shall give written notice of such pledge or assignment to the board of directors.

8. FIDUCIARIES AND JOINT OWNERS. An executor, administrator, guardian or trustee may vote, in person or by proxy, at any meeting of the Association with respect to any unit owned or held by him in such capacity, whether or not the same shall have been transferred to his name; provided, that he shall satisfy the secretary that he is the executor, administrator, guardian or trustee, holding such unit in such capacity. Whenever any unit is owned by two or more persons jointly, according to the records of the Association, the vote of such unit may be exercised by any one of the owners then present, in the absence of protest by a co-owner. In the event of such protest, no one co-owner shall be entitled to vote without the approval of all co-owners. In the event of disagreement among the co-owners, the vote of such unit shall be dis-

regarded completely in determining the proportion of votes given with respect to such matter.

9. QUORUM OF UNIT OWNERS. At any meeting of the Association, fifty percent (50) of the unit owners, present in person or by proxy, shall constitute a quorum. When a quorum is once present to organize a meeting, it cannot be broken by the subsequent withdrawal of a unit owner or owners. If any meeting of members cannot be organized because of a lack of quorum, the members who are present, either in person or by proxy, may adjourn the meeting from time to time until a quorum is present. At such adjourned meeting, at which a quorum is present or represented, any business may be transacted which might have been transacted at the meeting as originally noticed.

10. MAJORITY VOTE. The vote of more than fifty percent (50%) of the unit owners, comcomputed as provided in Article IX, Section 4(b), of these bylaws, present in person or by proxy, at a meeting at which a quorum is constituted shall be binding upon all unit owners for all purposes, except where a higher percentage vote is required by law, by the declaration, or by these bylaws.

11. ORDER OF BUSINESS. The order of business at annual meetings of the Association shall be:

    (a) Calling of the roll and certifying of proxies;
    (b) Proof of notice of meeting or waiver of notice;
    (c) Reading of minutes of preceding meeting;
    (d) Reports of officers;
    (e) Reports of committees, if any;
    (f) Election of directors;
    (g) Unfinished business;
    (h) New business; and
    (i) Adjournment.

ARTICLE III: BOARD OF DIRECTORS

1. NUMBER AND QUALIFICATION. The affairs of the Association shall be governed by a board of directors composed of from three (3) to five (5) persons as provided in Sections 2 and 3 of this Article. All directors, other than interim directors appointed by developer, shall be owners or co-owners of units of the condominium. For purposes of this section, the officers of the corporation and the partners of any partnership shall be considered co-owners of any units owned by such corporation or partnership.

2. INTERIM DIRECTORS. Upon the filing of the declaration submitting the condominium to the Oregon Unit Ownership Law, the developer shall apopoint an interim board of three (3) directors, who shall be Class A directors and serve until their successors have been elected by the unit owners as hereinafter provided.

3. ELECTION AND TERM OF OFFICE. At the first annual meeting, two Class B directors shall be elected to serve for a one-year term, thereby increasing the board to five (5) members. At each annual meeting thereafter until sixty percent (60%) of the units in the last phase of the condominium have been sold, successor Class B directors shall be elected for one-year terms. At the next annual meeting after 60 percent of the units in the final phase of development has been sold, the Class A interim directors shall resign and their successors shall be elected for two-year terms. The term of the then existing Class B directors shall be extended for an additional year until the next annual meeting, at which time their successors shall be elected for a two-year term. Thereafter, at the expiration of the initial term of office of each respective director, his successor shall be elected to serve for a term of two years, so that the term of not less than one third of the directors shall expire annually. Directors shall hold office

until their respective successors have been elected by the unit owners. Election shall be by plurality, computed in accordance with Article IX, Section 4(b) of these bylaws.

4. ADMINISTRATIVE RESPONSIBILITY. The unit owners shall assume full administrative responsibility of the condominium at the next annual meeting after 60 percent of the units in the final phase of development has been sold, the Class A interim directors shall have resigned and their successors, elected.

5. VACANCIES. Vacancies in the board of directors caused by any reason other than the removal of a director by a vote of the Association shall be filled by vote of the majority of the remaining directors, even though they may constitute less than a quorum, or by a sole remaining director. Each person so elected shall be a director until a successor is elected to fill the unexpired term at the next annual meeting of the Association or the next special meeting of the Association called for the purpose. Vacancies of Class A interim directors, however, shall be filled by developer.

6. REMOVAL OF DIRECTORS. At any regular or special meeting of the Association duly called, any one or more of the directors, other than interim directors, may be removed with or without cause by a majority vote of the unit owners present in person or by proxy, and a successor shall be elected at that meeting to fill the vacancy thus created. The notice of any such meeting shall state that such removal is to be considered, and any director whose removal has been proposed shall be given an opportunity to be heard at the meeting.

7. POWERS AND DUTIES. The board of directors shall have all of the powers and duties necessary for the administration of the affairs of the Association, except such powers and duties as by law or by the declaration or by these bylaws may not be delegated to the board of directors by the Association. The powers and

duties to be exercised by the board of directors shall include, but shall not be limited to, the following:

(a) Operation, care, upkeep, maintenance and repair of the general and limited common elements and Association property.

(b) Determination of the amounts required for operation, maintenance and other affairs of the Association, and the making of such expenditures.

(c) Collection of the common expenses from the unit owners.

(d) Employment and dismissal of such personnel as necessary for the efficient maintenance, upkeep and repair of the common elements and Association property.

(e) Employment of legal, accounting or other personnel for reasonable compensation to perform such services as may be required for the proper administration of the Association.

(f) Opening of bank accounts on behalf of the Asociation and designating the signatories required therefor.

(g) Purchasing units of the condominium at foreclosure or other judicial sales in the name of the Association or its designee, on behalf of all the unit owners as provided in these bylaws.

(h) Selling, leasing, mortgaging, voting the votes appurtenant to (other than for the election of directors), or otherwise dealing with, units of the condominium acquired by the Association or its designee on behalf of all the unit owners.

(i) Obtaining insurance or bonds pursuant to the provisions of these bylaws.

(j) Making additions and improvements to, or alterations of, the common elements and Association property; provided, however, that no such project may be undertaken by the board if the total cost will exceed the amount of $2,500.00, unless the unit owners have enacted a resolution authorizing the project by a vote of seventy-five percent (75%) of the unit owners present in person or by proxy at a meeting at which a quorum is constituted.

(k) Enforcement by legal means of the provisions of the Oregon Unit Ownership Law, the declarations filed thereunder, these bylaws and any rules and regulations adopted hereunder.

(l) Incorporation of the Association pursuant to the Oregon non-profit corporation law and the adoption of these bylaws as the bylaws of such corporation.

(m) In addition, the board of directors from time to time may adopt, modify or revoke such rules and regulations governing the conduct of persons and the operation and use of the units and common elements and Association property as it may deem necessary or appropriate in order to assure the peaceful and orderly use and enjoyment of the condominium property. Such action may be modified by vote of not less than seventy percent (70%) of the unit owners present, in person or by proxy, at any meeting, the notice of which shall have stated that such modification or revocation of rules and regulations will be under consideration. A copy of the rules and regulations, upon adopting, and a copy of each amendment, modification or revocation thereof, shall be delivered by the secretary promptly to each unit owner and shall be binding upon all unit owners and occupants of all units from the date of delivery.

8. MANAGING AGENT OR MANAGER. On behalf of the Association, the board of directors may employ or contract for a managing agent or a manager at a compensation to be established by the board of directors, which compensation shall constitute common expense. The board of directors may delegate to the managing agent or manager such duties and powers as the board of directors may authorize. In the absence of such appointment, the board of directors shall

act as manager.

9. ORGANIZATION MEETING. Within thirty (30) days following the annual meeting of the Association or following any meeting at which an election of directors has been held, the board of directors shall hold an organization meeting at such place and time as shall have been fixed by the directors at the meeting at which the election was held.

10. REGULAR AND SPECIAL MEETINGS. Regular meetings of the board of directors may be held at such time and place as shall be determined, from time to time, by a majority of the directors. Special meetings of the board of directors may be called by the chairman and must be called by the secretary at the written request of at least two directors. Notice of any spe-special meeting shall be given to each director, personally or by mail, telephone or telegraph at least seven (7) days prior to the day named for such meeting. However, if a majority of the units are the principal residences of the occupants, for other than emergency meetings, notice of the board of directors' meetings shall be posted at a place or places on the property at least three days prior to the meeting, or notice shall be provided by a method otherwise reasonably calculated to in-inform unit owners of such meetings. Emergency meetings of the board of directors may be conducted by telephone communication. All meetings of the board of directors of the Association shall be open to unit owners.

11. WAIVER OF NOTICE. Any director may, at any time, waive notice of any meeting of the board of directors in writing, and such waiver shall be deemed equivalent to the giving of such notice. Attendance by a director at any meeting of the board shall constitute a waiver by him of notice of the time and place thereof, except where a director attends the meeting for the express purpose of objecting to the transaction of any business because the

meeting is not lawfully called or convened.

12. QUORUM OF BOARD OF DIRECTORS. At all meetings of the board of directors, a majority of the directors shall constitute a quorum for the transaction of business, and the votes of a majority of the directors present at a meeting at which a quorum is present shall constitute the decision of the board of directors. If at any meeting of the board of directors, less than a quorum should be present, a majority of those present may adjourn the meeting from time to time. At any such adjourned meeting at which a quorum is present, any business which might have been transacted at the meeting originally called may be transacted without further notice.

13. PRESUMPTION OF ASSENT. A director who is present at a meeting of the board of directors at which action on any matter is taken shall be presumed to have assented to the action taken, unless his dissent shall be entered in the minutes of the meeting, or unless he shall file his written dissent to such action with the person acting as the secretary of the meeting before the adjournment thereof, or shall forward such dissent by registered mail to the secretary immediately after the adjournment of the meeting. Such right to dissent shall not apply to a director who voted in favor of such action.

14. COMPENSATION. No director shall receive any compensation from the Association for acting as such.

15. LIABILITY AND INDEMNIFICATION OF DIRECTORS, MANAGER, OR MANAGING AGENT. The directors shall not be liable to the Association for any mistake of judgment, negligence or otherwise except for their own willful misconduct or bad faith. The Association shall indemnify and hold harmless each director and the manager or managing agent, if any, against all contractual liability to others arising out of contracts made by the board of direc-

tors, manager or managing agent on behalf of the Association unless any such contract shall have been made in bad faith or contrary to the provisions of the declaration or of these bylaws. Each director and the manager or managing agent, if any, shall be indemnified by the Association against all expenses and liabilities, including attorneys' fees, reasonably incurred or imposed upon them in connection with any proceeding to which they may be a party, or in which they may become involved, by reason of being or having been a director, manager or managing agent, and shall be indemnified upon any reasonable settlement thereof; provided, however, there shall be no indemnity if the director, manager or managing agent is adjudged guilty of willful nonfeasance, misfeasance or malfeasance in the performance of his or her duties.

16. FIDELITY BONDS. The board of directors shall require that any person or entity, including but not limited to, employees of any professional manager who handles or is responsible for Association funds shall furnish such fidelity bond as the board deems adequate. The premiums on such bonds shall be paid by the Association.

17. INSURANCE. The board of directors shall obtain such liability insurance as the board deems necessary to protect the Association, its officers or employees and the unit owners. In addition, the board of directors, as trustee for the unit owners, shall obtain such casualty insurance as necessary to protect the entire condominium property. The board of directors, in its discretion, may obtain such other insurance as it deems necessary to protect the interests of the Association or unit owners. The board of directors shall conduct an annual insurance review which shall include an appraisal of all improvements contained in the condominium. No unit owner may engage in any activity which might jeopardize the in-

surance coverage described herein. Insurance policies obtained hereunder shall be master policies insuring the Association, its officers and directors, the manager or managing agent, if any, and unit owners and their mortgagees, as their respective interests may appear, and shall include the following provisions, if possible:

(a) Casualty coverage shall include those risks covered by a standard fire insurance policy with extended coverage endorsement and shall be for the full replacement cost without deduction of depreciation.

(b) Such policy shall contain a waiver of the usual proration clause, elimination of the usual "no other insurance" provision, and waiver of any right of subrogation as against any coinsured.

(c) Such policy shall require the insurance company to give notice of cancellation to the insureds and any mortgagees covered by loss payable clauses.

(d) Such policy shall bear a mortgagee's clause or a loss-payable clause in favor of any mortgagee or lender requesting the same, but such clause shall not give the mortgagee or lender the right to preempt payment of the insurance proceeds to the Association or to control whether or not the damage is repaired. The insurer shall likewise waive its right to determine whether the damage should be repaired, and loss adjustment and control of the proceeds of the policy shall rest in the Association as trustee for the unit owners.

(e) Liability coverage should cover any unit owner for his acts or omissions in connection with the condominium and cover any liability arising out of ownership of any unit of the condominium, and should contain a severability of interests provision so as to cover one unit owner for his liability to another unit owner.

ARTICLE IV: OFFICERS

1. DESIGNATION. The principal officers of the Association shall be the chairman, the secretary and the treasurer, all of whom shall be elected by the board of directors. The directors may appoint a vice-chairman, an assistant treasurer, an assistant secretary, and such other officers as in their judgment may be necessary. The chairman and vice-chairman shall be members of the board of directors, but the other officers need not be directors or unit owners. One person may hold more than one office, except the chairman and vice-chairman, who shall hold no other office.

2. ELECTION OF OFFICERS. The officers of the Association shall be elected annually by the board of directors at the organization meeting of each new board and shall hold office at the pleasure of the board. If any office shall become vacant, the board of directors shall elect a sucessor to fill the unexpired term at any regular meeting of the board of directors or at any special meeting of the board of directors called for such purpose.

3. REMOVAL OF OFFICERS. Upon the affirmative vote of a majority of the directors, any officer may be removed either with or without cause, and his successor may be elected at any regular meeting of the board of directors, or at any special meeting of the board of directors called for such purpose.

4. CHAIRMAN. The chairman shall be the chief executive officer of the Association. He shall preside at all meetings of the Association and of the board of directors. He shall have all of the general powers and duties which are usually vested in the chief executive officer of an association, including but not limited to the power to appoint committees from among the unit owners from time to time as he may in his discretion decide is appropriate to assist in the conduct of the affairs of the Association.

5. SECRETARY. The secretary shall keep the minutes of all proceedings of the board of directors and the minutes of all meetings of the Association. He shall attend to the giving and serving of all notices to the unit owners and directors and other notices required by law. He shall keep the records of the Association, except those of the treasurer, and shall perform all other duties incident to the office of secretary of an association and as may be required by the directors or the chairman.

6. TREASURER. The treasurer shall have the responsibility for Association funds and securities, for keeping full and accurate financial records and books of account showing all receipts and disbursements, and for the preparation of required financial statements. He shall be responsible for the deposit of all moneys and other valuable effects in such depositories as may from time to time be designated by the board of directors, and he shall disburse funds of the Association upon properly authorized vouchers. He shall perform all other duties incident to the office of treasurer of an association and such other duties as may be assigned to him by the board of directors.

7. EXECUTION OF INSTRUMENTS. All agreements, contracts, deeds, leases and other instruments of the Association, except checks, shall be executed by such person or persons as may be designated by general or special resolution of the board of directors, but in the absence of any general or special resolution applicable to any such instrument, the instrument shall be signed by the chairman and secretary. All checks shall be signed by the treasurer or, in his absence or disability, by the chairman or any duly-elected assistant treasurer.

8. COMPENSATION OF OFFICERS. No officer who is a member of the board of directors shall receive any compensation from the Association for acting as an officer, unless such compen-

sation is authorized by a resolution duly adopted by the unit owners. The board of directors may fix any compensation to be paid to other officers.

ARTICLE V: BUDGET, EXPENSES AND ASSESSMENTS

1. BUDGET. The board of directors shall from time to time, and at least annually, prepare a budget for the association, estimate the common expenses expected to be incurred, less any previous overassessment, and assess the common expenses to each unit owner in the same proportion as his percentage interest in the common elements. The board of directors shall advise each unit owner in writing of the amount of common expenses payable by him and furnish copies of each budget on which such common expenses are based to all unit owners and, if requested, to their mortgagees.

2. DETERMINATION OF COMMON EXPENSES. Common expenses shall include:
    (a) Expenses of administration.
    (b) Expenses of maintenance, repair, or replacement of common elements and Association property.
    (c) Cost of insurance or bonds obtained in accordance with these bylaws.
    (d) Charges for common utility meters.
    (e) A general operating reserve.
    (f) Reserve for replacements and deferred maintenance.
    (g) Any deficit in common expenses for any prior period.
    (h) Any other items properly chargeable as an expense of the Association.

3. ASSESSMENT OF COMMON EXPENSES. All unit owners shall be obliged to pay common expenses assessed to them by the board of directors on behalf of the Association pursuant to these bylaws and the declaration. The developer shall be assessed as the unit owner of any unsold unit, but such assessment shall be prorated to the date of sale of the unit. The board

of directors, on behalf of the Association, shall assess the common espenses against the unit owners from time to time, and at least annually, and shall take prompt action to collect from a unit owner any common expense due which remains unpaid by him for more than thirty (30) days from the due date for its payment. If additional units are annexed to the condominium, the board of directors shall promptly prepare a new budget reflecting the addition to the condominium and shall recompute any previous assessment covering any period after the annexation.

4. SPECIAL ASSESSMENTS.

(a) Capital Improvements. In the case of any duly authorized capital improvement to the common elements or Association property, the board of directors may by resolution establish separate assessments for the same, which may be treated as capital contributions by the unit owners, and the proceeds of which shall be used only for the specific capital improvements described in the resolution.

(b) Reserve Trust Funds. In establishing reserves for the maintenance, repair or replacement of the common elements or Association property, the board of directors may elect by resolution to establish one or more trust funds for the maintenance, repair or replacement of specific items, in which case the board shall either designate part of the regular assessment or establish separate assessments for such purposes. The proceeds therefrom shall be held in such trust funds and used only for the designated maintenance, repairs or replacements.

5. DEFAULT IN PAYMENT OF COMMON EXPENSES. In the event of default by any unit owner in paying to the Association the assessed common expenses, such unit owner shall be obligated to pay interest at the rate of nine percent (9%) per annum on such common expenses from the due date thereof, together with all ex-

penses, including attorneys' fees incurred by the Association in any proceeding brought to collect such unpaid expenses or any appeal therefrom. The board of directors shall have the right and duty to recover for the Association such common expenses, together with interest thereon, and expenses of the proceeding, including attorneys' fees, by an action brought against such unit owner or by foreclosure of the lien upon the unit granted by the Oregon Unit Ownership Law. The board of directors shall notify the holder of any first mortgage upon a unit of any default not cured within thirty (30) days of the date of default.

6. FORECLOSURE OF LIENS FOR UNPAID COMMON EXPENSES. In a suit brought by the Association to foreclose a lien on a unit because of unpaid common expenses, the unit owner shall be required to pay a reasonable rental for the use of the unit during the pendency of the suit, and the plaintiff in such foreclosure suit shall be entitled to the appointment of a receiver to collect such rental. The board of directors, acting on behalf of the Association, shall have the power to purchase such unit at the foreclosure sale and to acquire, hold, lease, mortgage, vote the votes appurtenant to, convey or otherwise deal with the unit. A suit or action to recover a money judgment for unpaid common expenses shall be maintainable without foreclosing the liens securing the same.

7. STATEMENT OF COMMON EXPENSES. The board of directors shall promptly provide any unit owner who makes a request in writing, with a written statement of his unpaid common expenses.

ARTICLE VI: RECORDS AND AUDITS

1. GENERAL RECORDS. The board of directors and the managing agent or manager, if any, shall keep detailed records of the actions of

the board of directors and the managing agent or manager, minutes of the meetings of the board of directors and minutes of the meetings of the Association. The board of directors shall maintain a list of owners entitled to vote at meetings of the Association and a list of all mortgagees of units.

2. RECORDS OF RECEIPTS AND EXPENDITURES. The board of directors or its designee shall keep detailed, accurate records in chronological order of the receipts and expenditures affecting the common elements and Association property, itemizing the maintenance and repair expenses of the common elements and Association property and any other expenses incurred. Such records and the vouchers authorizing the payments shall be available for examination by the unit owners and mortgagees at convenient hours of weekdays.

3. ASSESSMENT ROLL. The assessment roll shall be maintained in a set of accounting books in which there shall be an account for each unit. Such account shall designate the name and address of the owner or owners, the amount of each assessment against the owners, the dates and amounts in which the assessment comes due, the amounts paid upon the account and the balance due on the assessments.

4. PAYMENT OF VOUCHERS. The treasurer shall pay all vouchers up to $1,000 signed by the chairman, managing agent, manager or other person authorized by the board of directors. Any voucher in excess of $1,000 shall require the signature of the chairman.

5. REPORTS AND AUDITS. An annual report of the receipts and expenditutes of the Association shall be rendered by the board of directors to all unit owners and to all mortgagees of units who have requested the same within 90 days after the end of each fiscal year. From time to time the board of directors, at the expense of the Association, may obtain an audit of the books and records pertaining to the

Association and furnish copies thereof to the owners and such mortgagees. At any time any owner or mortgagee may, at his own expense, cause an audit or inspection to be made of the books and records of the Association.

6. NOTICE OF SALE, MORTGAGE OR LEASE. Immediately upon the sale, mortgage, or lease of any unit, the unit owner shall promtly inform the secretary or manager of the name and address of said vendee, mortgagee or lessee.

ARTICLE VII: MAINTENANCE AND USE OF CONDOMINIUM PROPERTY

1. MAINTENANCE AND REPAIR. Except as otherwise provided herein for damage or destruction caused by casualty:

(a) Units. All maintenance of and repairs to any unit shall be made by the owner of such unit, who shall keep the same in good order, condition and repair and shall do all redecorating, painting and staining which at any time may be necessary to maintain the good appearance and condition of his unit. In addition, each unit owner shall be responsible for the maintenance, repair or replacement of windows and doors and the baseboard heating units, any plumbing fixtures, telephones, water heaters, fans, lighting fixtures and lamps, fireplaces, refrigerators, dishwashers, ranges or other appliances and accessories that may be in or connected with his unit.

(b) Common elements and Association property. All maintenance, repairs and replacements to the general and limited common elements and Association property, including, without limitation, repair and replacement of the roof and restaining or painting of the exterior of the buildings, shall be made by the Association and shall be charged to all the unit owners as a common expense. Each unit owner, however, shall keep the limited common elements which pertain to his unit in a neat, clean and sanitary condition.

2. ADDITIONS, ALTERATIONS OR IMPROVEMENTS. A unit owner shall not, without first obtaining written consent of the board of directors, make or permit to be made any structural alteration, improvement or addition in or to his unit, or in or to the exterior of the buildings or any other general or limited common elements or Association property. A unit owner shall make no repair or alteration or perform any other work on his unit which would jeopardize the soundness or safety of the property, or reduce the value thereof or impair any easement or hereditament unless the written consent of all unit owners affected is obained. A unit owner shall not paint or decorate any portion of the exterior of the buildings or other general or limited common elements without first obtaining written consent of the board of directors.

3. DAMAGE OR DESTRUCTION BY CASUALTY OF CONDOMINIUM PROPERTY.

(a) In the event of damage or destruction by casualty of condominium property, the damage or destruction shall be repaired, reconstructed or rebuilt unless, within fourteen (14) days of such damage or destruction, the board of directors or more than ten percent (10%) of the unit owners shall have requested a special meeting of the Association. Such special meeting must be held within sixty (60) days of the date of damage or destruction. At the time of such meeting, unless ninety percent (90%) of the unit owners, whether in person, by writing or by proxy, vote not to repair, reconstruct or rebuild the damaged property, the damage or destruction shall be repaired, reconstructed or rebuilt. In the case of substantial damage or destruction, timely written notice thereof shall be given to the unit owners and their mortgagees.

(b) The Association shall be responsible for repairing, reconstructing or rebuilding all such damage or destruction to the common elements and, to the extent of the Association's insurance coverage, all such damage or destruction to the units. Each unit owner shall be responsible for such repairing, reconstructing or rebuilding of his unit as is not covered by the Association's insurance.

(c) If, due to the act or neglect of a unit owner, or of a member of his family or his household pet or of a guest or other authorized occupant or visitor of such unit owner, damage shall be caused to the common elements or to a unit owned by others, or maintenance, repairs or replacements shall be reequired which would otherwise be a common expense, then such unit owner shall pay for such damage and such maintenance, repairs and replacements as may be determined by the Association, to the extent not covered by the Association's insurance.

(d) In the event the insurance proceeds paid to the Association are not used to repair, reconstruct or rebuild the damaged or destroyed property, the Association shall distribute the proceeds among the unit owners and their mortgagees (as their interests may appear) in the same proportion as their respective undivided interests in the common elements as determined by ORS.

4. CONDEMNATION. In the event of a taking in condemnation by eminent domain of part or all of the common elements or Association property, the award made for such taking shall be payable to the Association. If such proceedings are instituted or such acquisition is sought by a condemning authority as to any portion of the property, prompt notice thereof shall be given to the unit owners and their mortgagees. If seventy-five percent (75%) or more of the unit owners duly and promptly approve the repair or restoration of such common elements or Association property, the board of directors shall arrange for the same, which shall be paid out of the proceeds of the

award. In the event seventy-five percent (75%) or more of the unit owners do not duly and promptly approve the repair and restoration of such common elements or Association property, the board of directors shall disburse the net proceeds of such award to the unit owners and their mortgagees (as their interests may appear) in the same proportions as the respective and undivided interests of the unit owners in the common elements as determined by ORS.

5. MARINA.

(a) Within 30 days after adjournment of the first organizational meeting of the Association, pursuant to Article II, Section 2, of these bylaws, the Developer will transfer the Submerged and Submersible Lands Lease pertaining to the marina (provided consent to the transfer can be obtained from the State of Oregon), and transfer ownership of the marina and related facilities and equipment ("marina") to the Association.

(b) Thereafter the marina shall be the property of the Association available for such use as the Association may deem appropriate subject to the provisions of the declaration and these bylaws.

(c) The unit owners shall have first opportunity to lease slips in the marina for the fee set by the Association when the Association makes them available for lease. After every unit owner has had an opportunity to lease one slip for each unit owned, the Association may then make the slips available for lease, for the fee set by the Association, by persons not unit owners for terms not to exceed one year. At the end of each lease period for slips leased to persons not unit owners, such slips shall then become available for lease in the following order: (1) to unit owners not then leasing a slip for each unit owned; (2) to other persons not unit owners, if the Association decides to continue to lease slips to persons not unit owners.

6. RESTRICTIONS AND REQUIREMENTS RESPECTING USE OF CONDOMINIUM PROPERTY. The following restrictions and requirements are in addition to all other restrictions and requirements contained in the declaration and these bylaws:

(a) Residential use. No commercial activities of any kind shall be carried on in any unit or in any other portion of the condominium without the consent of the board of directors of the Association or manager, except activities relating to the rental or sale of units. This provision, however, shall not be construed so as to prevent or prohibit a unit owner from maintaining his professional personal library, keeping his personal business or profesional records or accounts, handling his personal business or professional telephone calls or conferring with business or professional associates, clients or customers, in his unit.

(b) Use of common elements. The common elements shall be used for the furnishing of services and facilities for which the same are reasonably intended for the enjoyment of the units. The use, operation and maintenance of the common elements shall not be obstructed, damaged or unreasonably interfered with by any unit owner.

(c) Offensive or unlawful activities. No noxious or offensive activities shall be carried on in any unit, nor shall anything be done or placed upon any unit which interferes with or jeopardizes the enjoyment of other units or the common elements or which is a source of annoyance to residents. No unlawful use shall be made of the condominium nor any part thereof, and all valid laws, zoning ordinances and regulations of all governmental bodies having jurisdiction thereof shall be observed.

(d) Animals. No animals or fowls shall be raised, kept or permitted within the condominium or any part thereof except domestic dogs, cats or other household pets kept within a unit or on a leash at all times when within the condominium. No such dogs, cats or pets shall be permitted to run at large nor shall be kept, bred or raised for commercial purposes or in unreasonable numbers. Any inconvenience, damage or unpleasantness caused by such pets shall be the responsibility of the respective owners thereof.

(e) Exterior lighting or noisemaking devices. Except with the consent of the board of directors of the Association or manager, no exterior lighting or noisemaking devices shall be installed or maintained on any unit.

(f) Windows, balconies and outside walls. In order to preserve the attractive appearance of the condominium, the board of directors of the Association or the manager may regulate the nature of items which may be placed in or on windows, balconies, decks, porches, entryways, carports and the outside walls so as to be visible from other units, the common elements or outside the condominium.

(g) Trailers and boats. Except with the consent of the board of directors of the Association or manager, no travel trailer, boat or boat trailer, or other recreational vehicles, other motor homes and campers installed on trucks shall be parked on any portion of the condominium.

(h) Leasing and rental of units. Except with the consent of the board of dirctors of the Association or the manager, no unit owner may lease or rent less than his entire unit, and such unit shall not be leased or rented to any tenant for a period of less than thirty (30) days. Other than the foregoing, there is no restriction on the right of any unit owner to lease or rent his unit.

(i) Garbage and refuse disposal. No trash, garbage or other waste shall be placed or kept outside of any unit, except in sanitary containers designated for such purpose for the common use of all unit owners.

(j) Speed limit. The speed limit on all roadways within the condominium shall be ten miles per hour.

(k) Laundry, rugs, etc. No garments, rugs, laundry or other similar items shall be hung from windows, patios or other external structures. It is prohibited to dust rugs or similar items from the windows or to clean rugs or similar items by beating on the exterior part of any building.

(l) Wiring, antennas, etc. No unit owner may install wiring for electrical or telephone installation, television antenna, radio antenna, grills, machines, or air conditioning units, or similar devices on the exterior of a unit or that protrude through the walls or the roof of a unit, except as authorized in writing by the board of directors.

(m) Parking areas. There shall be no storage of materials of any kind in areas designated for parking, except motor vehicles. No parking area shall be used as a parking place for motor vehiches not in regular family use and good operating condition.

(n) Signs. Unless written approval is first obtained from the board of directors, no sign of any kind shall be displayed to the public view on any unit except signs used by the Developer to advertise units for sale during the construction and sales period.

7. RIGHT OF ENTRY. A unit owner shall grant the right of entry to the board of directors, managing agent, manager or any other person authorized by the board of directors in the case of an emergency originating in or threatening his unit or other condominium property, whether or not the owner is present at the time. A unit owner shall also permit such persons to enter his unit for the purpose of performing installation, alterations or repairs to any common element and for the pur-

pose of performing installation, alterations or repairs to any common element and for the purpose of inspection to verify that the unit owner is complying with the restrictions and requirements described in Section 5 of this Article, provided that requests for entry are made in advance and that such entry is at a time convenient to the owner.

8. EASEMENTS FOR DEVELOPER. Developer and its agents, successors and assigns shall have an easement over and upon the common elements for the purpose of constructing additional phases, making repairs to existing structures and carrying out sales and rental activities necessary or convenient for the sale or rental of units, including, without limitation, the right to use the units owned by developer or its agent as model units or as a sales office.

9. ABATEMENT AND ENJOINING OF VIOLATIONS. The violation of any rule or regulation adopted hereunder or the breach of any bylaw contained herein or of any provision of the declaration shall give the board of directors, acting on hehalf of the Association, the right, in addition to any other rights set forth in these bylaws:

(a) to enter the unit in which or as to which such violation exists and to summarily abate and remove, at the expense of the defaulting unit owner, any structure, thing, or condition that may exist therein contrary to the intent and meaning of the provisions hereof, and the board of directors shall not thereby be deemed guilty of any manner of trespass; or

(b) to enjoin, abate, or remedy such thing or condition by appropriate legal proceedings.

ARTICLE VIII: AMENDMENTS TO BYLAWS

1. HOW PROPOSED. Amendments to the bylaws shall be proposed by either a majority of the board of directors or by thirty percent (30%)

of the unit owners. The proposed amendment must be reduced to writing and shall be included in the notice of any meeting at which action is to be taken thereon.

2. ADOPTION. A resolution adopting a proposed amendment may be proposed by either the board of directors or by the unit owners as aforesaid and may be approved by the unit owners at a meeting called for this purpose. Unit owners not present at the meeting considering such amendment may express their approval in writing or by proxy. Any resolution must be approved by seventy-five percent (75%) of the unit owners.

3. EXECUTION AND RECORDING. An amendment shall not be effective until certified by the chairman and secretary of the Association, approved by the Oregon Real Estate Commissioner and recorded as required by law.

ARTICLE IX: MISCELLANEOUS

1. NOTICES. All notices to the Association or to the board of directors shall be sent care of the managing agent or, if there is no managing agent, to the principal office of the Association or to such other address as the board of directors may hereafter designate from time to time. All notices to any unit owner shall be sent to such address as may have been designated by him from time to time, in writing, to the board of dirctors or, if no address has been designated, then to the owner's unit.

2. WAIVER. No restriction, condition, obligation, or provision contained in these bylaws shall be deemed to have been abrogated or waived by reason of any failure to enforce the same, irrespective of the number of violations or breaches thereof which may occur.

3. INVALIDITY; NUMBER; CAPTIONS. The invalidity of any part of these bylaws shall not impair or affect in any manner the validity, enforceability or effect of the balance of

these bylaws. As used herein, the singular shall include the plural, and the plural, the singular. The masculine and neuter shall each include the masculine, feminine and neuter as the context requires. All captions used herein are intended solely for convenience or reference and shall in no way limit any of the provisions of these bylaws.

4. DEFINITIONS.

(a) Adoption by reference. The definitions contained in or adopted by the declaration shall be applicable to these bylaws.

INDEX

Abatement, 160
Absenteeism, 71
Adoption of bylaws, 127
Administration, 31, 34
Agenda, 21, 22
Allocation of common expenses, 111
Alteration, 112, 153
Analysis ledger, 31, 83, 84
Animals, 55, 157
Arguments, 68
Assessments, 149, 150-52
Association, 13, 21, 26, 27, 41, 53, 61, 63
   Insurance, 45-49
   Meetings, 135-38
Balance sheet, 22, 31, 91, 92
Board of directors, 21, 25, 26, 27
   Election of, 139
   Insurance, 45-48
   Interim, 139
   Management, 31-33, 41
   Number of, 139
   Powers of, 140
   Records required, 151-52
   Removals in, 140
   Responsibilities of, 140
   Restrictions by, 156-59
   Vacancies in, 140
Boat trailers, 69
Bookkeeping, 26, 31, 40, 41, 55, 64, 79
Boundaries of unit, 109, 124
Budget, 22, 26, 31, 54, 55, 63, 70, 85
   And expenses, 149-51
   Preparation of, 85-87, 149
Bylaws, 17, 18, 23, 54, 55, 58
   Appendix C, 132-62
   Contents of (required by ORS), 106-07
   In the Declaration, 123, 127
   Insurance, 45-48
Chairman, 23, 26, 107
   Duties of, 147

Checkbook, 31, 79, 80
Committees, 21, 25, 26, 31
Common area, 13, 17, 45
Common expenses, 149-52
Common utilities, 56
Communication, 34, 73
Compensation, 144, 148
Complaints, 74
Condemnation, 155
Construction, 56, 57
Damage, 154
Declaration, 17, 18, 58, 123
Deed, 108
Deferred maintenance 31
Definitions, 123, 162
Developer, 54, 56, 61, 66, 72
Development, 17, 26, 53
Disclosure by developer, 114, 115
Dues, 27, 58-59, 83, 126
   Collection of, 35-40,
   Common expenses, 149-52
Easements, 105, 160
Emergencies, 73
Encroachments, 126
Fidelity bonds, 145
Finances, 54, 61
Floods, 49, 50
Foreclosure, 108, 109, 151
Garbage and grounds, 59, 158
General common elements, 124
Government, 21
Grounds, 26, 31, 33
Guidelines, 17, 34
Housing, 8, 13
Improvements, 8, 13
Income tax, 31, 55, 93, 94
Indemnification, 47, 48, 105, 144
Instruments, 148
Insurance, 13, 22, 27, 31, 32, 54
   By bylaws, 145-46
   By ORS, 108
   By rules, regulations and experience, 45-50
Interest in common elements, 110

Interim board, 127
Invalidity, 161
Keys, 74
Lateness, 61, 104
Laundry, 158
Leaks, 60
Legal help, 71
Lien, 22, 108
Lighting, 158
Limited common elements
Living, 97, 98
Maintenance, 26, 111, 112, 149, 153
   Kinds of, 31-33
   Problems of, 64-66
Management, 26, 48, 98, 103
   Composition, 31-35
   Types of, 40-41
Manager, 98, 109, 127, 142, 144
Marina 10, 54, 61, 62, 156
Meetings, 21,22
   Annual, 135
   Fiduciaries, 137
   First organizational, 135, 143
   Notice of, 136, 143
   Order of business, 138
   Special, 136, 143
Minutes, 22, 25. 26
Mortgagee approval, 127
Name and location, 134
Newsletter, 73
Noise, 34, 56, 62, 69, 158
Notices, 161
Numbering, 58
Offensive activities, 69, 157
Office, 135
Officers
   Chairman, 147
   Compensation, 148
   Designation, 146
   Election, 147
   Execution of instruments, 148
   Removal, 147
   Secretary, 147

Treasurer, 148
ORS, 45, 103
Outside appearance, 158
Parking, 34, 55, 56, 69, 159
Penalty, 22
Percentage interests, 17, 127
Plan of development, 128
Powers of Association, 103
Presumption of assent, 144
Profits and expenses, 126
Property, 123
Proxy, 23, 24, 137
Purposes of Association, 135
Quorum, 23, 138, 144
Real Estate Commissioner, 17
Records, 109
Recreation, 8
Rentals, 71, 72, 98, 158
Resales, 13
Reserve trust fund, 150
Restitutions, 53
Retirement, 8
Right of entry, 159
Roofing repair, 67
Sale cancellation, 118-20
Sale requirements, 117, 153
Sea wall, 25, 68
Secretary, 26, 55, 105, 107
   Duties of, 147
Security, 35, 74
Service of Process, 113, 126
Signs, 159
Speed limit, 158
Statement of expenses and income, 22, 31, 54, 86, 88
Statutes, 17, 18
Taxation, 113
Tenants, 45, 55
Tidal wave, 49
Trailers, 158
Treasurer, 22, 26, 54, 55, 107, 147
   Duties of, 148
Undivided interest, 13

Unit owner ledger, 31, 45, 46, 61, 152
  Details of, 81-82
Units, 27, 60, 62
  Construction, 56-58
  Declaration requirements, 124-130
  Insurance, 45-47
  Lien, 151
  ORS requirements, 108-120
Use of property, 125, 156
  Common elements, 157
  Residential, 157
Voting, 23, 126
  Details of, 136-38
Waiver, 161
Wiring, 159